D1519834

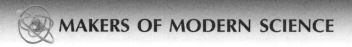

MAKERS OF MODERN SCIENCE

Chien-shiung Wu

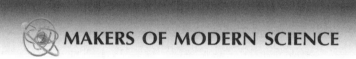

MAKERS OF MODERN SCIENCE

Chien-shiung Wu

Pioneering Nuclear Physicist

RICHARD HAMMOND, PH.D.

CHELSEA HOUSE
P U B L I S H E R S
An imprint of Infobase Publishing

CHIEN-SHIUNG WU: Pioneering Nuclear Physicist

Copyright © 2010 by Richard Hammond, Ph.D.

Chelsea House
An imprint of Infobase Publishing
132 West 31st Street
New York NY 10001

Library of Congress Cataloging-in-Publication Data

Hammond, Richard, 1950–
    Chien-shiung Wu: pioneering nuclear physicist / Richard Hammond.
      p. cm.
    Includes bibliographical references and index.
    ISBN-13: 978-0-8160-6177-8
    ISBN-10: 0-8160-6177-7
    1. Wu, C. S. (Chien-shiung), 1912–1997—Juvenile literature. 2. Nuclear physi-
cists—United States—Biography—Juvenile literature. 3. Nuclear physicists—
China—Biography—Juvenile literature. I. Title.
    QC774.W8H36 2010
    539.7092—dc22
[B]   2008054434

Text design by Kerry Casey
Cover design by Salvatore Luongo and Alicia Post
Illustrations by Sholto Ainslie
Photo research by Suzanne M. Tibor

Printed in the United States of America

MP KT 10 9 8 7 6 5 4 3 2 1

This book is printed on acid-free paper and contains 30 percent postconsumer recycled content.

CONTENTS

PREFACE

S cience is, above all, a great human adventure. It is the process of exploring what Albert Einstein called the "magnificent structure" of nature using observation, experience, and logic. Science comprises the best methods known to humankind for finding reliable answers about the unknown. With these tools, scientists probe the great mysteries of the universe—from black holes and star nurseries to deep-sea hydrothermal vents (and extremophile organisms that survive high temperatures to live in them); from faraway galaxies to subatomic particles such as quarks and antiquarks; from signs of life on other worlds to microorganisms such as bacteria and viruses here on Earth; from how a vaccine works to protect a child from disease to the DNA, genes, and enzymes that control traits and processes from the color of a boy's hair to how he metabolizes sugar.

Some people think that science is rigid and static, a dusty, musty set of facts and statistics to memorize for a test and then forget. Some think of science as antihuman—devoid of poetry, art, and a sense of mystery. However, science is based on a sense of wonder and is all about exploring the mysteries of life and our planet and the vastness of the universe. Science offers methods for testing and reasoning that help keep us honest with ourselves. As physicist Richard Feynman once said, science is above all a way to keep from fooling yourself—or letting nature (or others) fool you. Nothing could be more growth-oriented or more human. Science evolves continually. New bits of knowledge and fresh discoveries endlessly shed light and open perspectives. As a result, science is constantly undergoing revolutions—ever refocusing what scientists have explored before into fresh, new understanding. Scientists like to say science is self-correcting. That is, science is fallible, and scientists can be wrong. It is easy to fool yourself, and it is easy to be fooled by others, but because new facts are constantly flowing in, scientists are continually refining their work to account for as many facts as possible. So science can make mistakes, but it also can correct itself.

Sometimes, as medical scientist Jonas Salk liked to point out, good science thrives when scientists ask the right question about what they observe. "What people think of as the moment of discovery is really the discovery of the question," he once remarked.

There is no one, step-by-step "scientific method" that all scientists use. However, science requires the use of methods that are systematic, logical, and *empirical* (based on objective observation and experience). The goal of science is to explore and understand how nature works—what causes the patterns, the shapes, the colors, the textures, the consistency, the mass, and all the other characteristics of the natural universe that we see.

What is it like to be a scientist? Many people think of stereotypes of the scientist trapped in cold logic or the cartoonlike "mad" scientists. In general, these portrayals are more imagination than truth. Scientists use their brains. They are exceptionally good at logic and critical thinking. This is where the generalizations stop. Although science follows strict rules, it is often guided by the many styles and personalities of the scientists themselves, who have distinct individuality, personality, and style. What better way to explore what science is all about than through the experiences of great scientists?

Each volume of the Makers of Modern Science series presents the life and work of a prominent scientist whose outstanding contributions have garnered the respect and recognition of the world. These men and women were all great scientists, but they differed in many ways. Their approaches to the use of science were different: Niels Bohr was an atomic theorist whose strengths lay in patterns, ideas, and conceptualization, while Wernher von Braun was a hands-on scientist/engineer who led the team that built the giant rocket used by Apollo astronauts to reach the Moon. Some's genius was sparked by solitary contemplation—geneticist Barbara McClintock worked alone in fields of maize and sometimes spoke to no one all day long. Others worked as members of large, coordinated teams. Oceanographer Robert Ballard organized oceangoing ship crews on submersible expeditions to the ocean floor; biologist Jonas Salk established the

Salk Institute to help scientists in different fields collaborate more freely and study the human body through the interrelationships of their differing knowledge and approaches. Their personal styles also differed: biologist Rita Levi-Montalcini enjoyed wearing chic dresses and makeup; McClintock was sunburned and wore baggy denim jeans and an oversized shirt; nuclear physicist Richard Feynman was a practical joker and an energetic bongo drummer.

The scientists chosen represent a spectrum of disciplines and a diversity of approaches to science as well as lifestyles. Each biography explores the scientist's younger years along with education and growth as a scientist; the experiences, research, and contributions of the maturing scientist; and the course of the path to recognition. Each volume also explores the nature of science and its unique usefulness for studying the universe and contains sidebars covering related facts or profiles of interest, introductory coverage of the scientist's field, line illustrations and photographs, a time line, a glossary of related scientific terms, and a list of further resources including books, Web sites, periodicals, and associations.

The volumes in the Makers of Modern Science series offer a factual look at the lives and exciting contributions of the profiled scientists in the hope that readers will see science as a uniquely human quest to understand the universe and that some readers may be inspired to follow in the footsteps of these great scientists.

ACKNOWLEDGMENTS

I would like to thank Nancy, Katherine, Jennifer, and Matthew, without whose infinite patience this book could not have been written. I would also like to thank Frank Darmstadt, executive editor, and Jodie Rhodes, my literary agent, for their help and guidance.

INTRODUCTION

At the time of Chien-shiung Wu's birth in 1912, the world of physics was exploding with new and inexplicable observations and experiments. For example, scientists discovered that energy was emitted in patterns that could not be explained by the physics of the time. The new field of atomic physics was followed by the even more mysterious field of nuclear physics. In this context, the world generally clamored for more education, but in China, where Chien-shiung Wu was born, girls were not allowed to go to school. This prohibition makes it even more remarkable how she was able to rise to become one of the most preeminent experimental physicists in the world.

Thanks to her father, Wu Chung-i, she was able to go to his girls' school, one of the first founded in the country, and then on to the prestigious National Central University in Nanking (Nanjing) in 1930. But, this was not enough. Already fascinated by physics and eager to learn more, but with no graduate schools in her homeland, Wu struck out for the United States, arriving in California in 1936. Ernest Lawrence, a notable nuclear physicist who would later win the Nobel Prize for his invention of the cyclotron, had recently joined the physics department at the University of California at Berkeley. He was so impressed with Wu that he offered her a modest stipend to work there as a graduate student. This put Wu at the focus of the burgeoning field of nuclear physics—a field that would change our world.

When Japan invaded China, Wu felt very isolated in her new country. This circumstance only made her work harder, and as she said many times throughout her life, she took her father's advice to "ignore the obstacles. . . . Just put your head down and keep walking forward." She kept walking forward throughout her life, overcoming prejudice against women and against Asians. In fact, her hard work eventually led to Wu being invited to work on the most secret large-scale project the United States ever devised—the Manhattan Project, the mission that designed and tested the first atomic bomb ever made.

Chien-shiung Wu: Pioneering Nuclear Physicist will show how Wu established herself as a world-renowned experimentalist in nuclear physics. The reader will learn how she solved important challenges of the day, such as her improvements in radioactive detectors during World War II, and how she cleared up the mystery of beta decay.

Wu's devotion to hard work and long hours in the lab set an example for her students and made her reputation grow as an excellent experimentalist. So, when two top theoretical physicists, Tsung-Dao Lee and Chen Ning Yang, were thinking that a "fundamental truth" of physics might be wrong, they went to her to do the experiment.

Physicists sometimes live in a different world than most other people; they resort to a world of equations and fundamental laws where the only language allowed is mathematics. It is in this abstract world where physics makes sense, where fundamental issues can be framed with scientific accuracy and precision. Wu was able to thrive both in this conceptual world and the prosaic world of the laboratory, sprawling with wires and detectors and all the instruments that translate the theoretical world of mathematics to the real world of things we can measure.

Standing between these two extremes like a bridge was the concept of "parity." We will delve into the precise meaning of this concept later in this book, but for now we say this. Parity is the property that dictates whether nature looks the same if it is viewed directly or in a mirror. If parity is conserved, then things will look the same in the mirror, and for decades this was taken as gospel. Parity was conserved, and physicists were as faithful as ministers. This is the "fundamental truth" Lee and Yang came to question, and for which they asked Wu to do the experiment.

Wu never balked at hard work or a difficult challenge; in fact, she rejoiced in such a test. Lee and Yang did not even know if such an experiment could be performed, but Wu did it. She assembled a handpicked team of physicists and, after designing an experiment that brought the particles to the lowest temperatures possible, proved that parity is not conserved. In so doing, she overthrew a long-standing, erroneous belief.

Experiments as profound and important as this are extremely rare. Physicists come to believe in things through long and careful analysis, and to overturn a long-held belief takes courage. Wu had both the courage and ability to perform such an experiment and had gained a reputation so that her result was accepted.

This volume of the Makers of Modern Science set shows how Wu developed her extraordinary ability to test many laws of physics and how she gained her reputation. Having developed, from her childhood in China, the ability to "self-learn," this characteristic allowed her to "walk forward" throughout her life, thereby cutting new trails across the rugged landscape of experimental physics.

Notes

One: In order to explain the physics with which Chien-shiung Wu was working, special units are used in this book. Standard International (SI) and other related units are defined and used in the book. These are the units physicists use to explain their results.

Two: Chinese terms are transliterated according to the Wade-Giles system, with pinyin equivalent transliterations provided parenthetically, where appropriate.

1

The Atomic World

A t the dawn of the atomic and nuclear age, a girl was born on May 13, 1912, in Liu Ho (Liuhe), a small town in China 30 miles (48 km) from the thriving and bustling port city of Shanghai. The girl was the daughter of Wu Chung-i (Wu Zhongyi), principal of the school in her hometown. The girl would go well beyond this modest school, studying at one of the finest universities in the United States, and become one the greatest experimental nuclear physicists of her new country, thereby shattering the prevailing view of the world. The girl was Wu Chien-shiung (Wu Jianxong). (In China, it is custom to present surname first, followed by one's given name. In the United States, her name became Chien-shiung Wu, pronounced "Chyen shyung Woo.") Before her outstanding contributions can be appreciated, however, it is necessary to go back and understand what people used to think, to look at the world from the same perch as the people of her time did.

The China in which Wu was raised was a country that had recently gone through a revolution that ended the rule of dynasties and made the country a republic. Physics at the same time was going through its own revolution. Throughout Europe, physicists were embarking on a series of experiments that turned their view of the world upside down. As they struggled to learn and understand this new atomic physics, Wu was struggling to get an education, a difficult task for young girls in China at that time.

School in China

Wu excelled in her father's school. Each day, Wu would come home to a house filled with books, packed wall to wall in every space like an old bookstore. Invigorated from her daytime lessons, Wu would use these books at night and graduated at the top of her class. She did so well, in fact, that a small crisis engaged the Wu family when she was still very young. Although Wu Chung-i's little school would later expand, when Chien-shiung studied there it only had four elementary grades. Chien-shiung graduated when she was nine, and although her father wanted her to continue her education, there were no other schools in her small hometown of Liu Ho.

It is important to realize how different China in 1921 was from the United States today or even back then. Children growing up in the United States expect to go to school, for free, right up through the 12th grade. Schools are everywhere, usually within walking distance or at most a short bus ride from home. When someone finishes fifth or sixth grade, the biggest family discussion might be about which high school to attend. This is true for both boys and girls.

In China in Wu's time, young girls were still having their feet bound. This was a custom from the past that the new China was trying to end as antiquated and discriminatory. Another habit from the past was restricting education to only males, and so, sending a girl to school was something unusual. For this reason, Chien-shiung's father started his school for girls—to afford them an education that girls would otherwise not have had. This is probably the backdrop for the conversations in the Wu household when Chien-shiung was approaching 10 years old. She had always been at the top of her class, receiving the highest grades, but now the family had to face the dilemma of what to do with this precocious young girl who wanted to learn more?

Another difference between Chinese society and that of the United States is family structure and influence. In the United States, parents usually make all the decisions for their children. Although they may talk it over with other family members, parents usually decide matters that concern the future of their children. It was different in the Wu family. Chung-i conferred with his great-grandmother, who was well read even though she never went to school, and was the family matriarch. Her ruling was that the young girl must attend the best school possible, wherever it was. What a great decision this was, and the entire physics community has her to thank!

A friend of Wu Chung-i taught at a very good girls' school in Suchou (Suzhou), about 50 miles (80 km) away from Liu Ho, and he promised to look after Chien-shiung. She excelled there and developed the important ability of self-learning (learning about things she did not study in class). This was the equivalent of going to high school, and by the time she graduated at the age of 17, several major controversies were brewing in the United States and across the globe. In order to understand her contributions to physics, one must take a detour through the fascinating field of atomic and nuclear physics (see sidebar).

Chien-shiung Wu's passport picture (SPL/Photo Researchers, Inc.)

Radioactivity, a New Form of Energy

The dawn of the 20th century brought physics into a new age. The change was so striking the new era came to be called "modern physics," a name that is still used today, more than a century later. Before this, the field of physics covered two general areas: gravity, which describes everything from how a baseball flies through the air to how planets whirl around the Sun, and electromagnetism, a broad field that describes a wide range of phenomena, from how light speeds through air or vacuum, to the effects of a compass needle struggling to align with the Earth's magnetic field.

As the 19th century moved into the 20th, scientists worked diligently in the laboratory, creating new kinds of experiments that could not be explained by either gravity or electromagnetism. An entirely new set of laws, now known as modern physics, was at work, and no one could explain the bizarre measurements. For example, it was discovered that hydrogen emitted visible light at only four wavelengths, whereas classical electromagnetism predicted that hydrogen should emit light at all wavelengths. In another example, Ernest Rutherford (1871–1937), a noted English physicist, discovered that uranium, a heavy element, emitted new forms of energy. At this time, when all of the basic laws of physics dealt with gravity or electromagnetism, scientists were baffled. These new experiments, the basis of modern physics, began when physicists started to measure the energy bursting from this exotic material, finding that the radiation had little respect for the known laws of physics. To make things even more complicated, physicists found that uranium emitted different kinds of energy: One kind had a negative charge, like the charge on electrons, another had a positive charge, like the charge on a proton, and another form of energy had no charge at all!

By the turn of the 20th century, it was known that atoms were a few angstroms in diameter. An angstrom (Å) is one ten-billionth of a meter, which is articulated as 10^{-10} m. It was also known that an atom had equal and opposite amounts of charge. In the plum pudding model, the positive charge is the sweet center, and the electrons are stuck on the outside like tiny raisins.

Rutherford began a series of experiments to learn more about these new forms of energy and labeled the positively charged particles as alpha rays and the negatively charged particles as beta rays, and later the neutral form of energy was named gamma rays. (Alpha, beta, and gamma come from the first three letters in the Greek alphabet.) Rutherford came to know that the alpha rays were really the nuclei of helium atoms. The helium nucleus is made from two protons and two

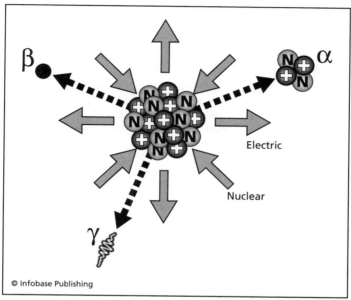

A radioactive nucleus can emit or absorb alpha, beta, or gamma rays.

neutrons. Since neutrons are neutral, the alpha particles were known to have exactly twice the charge of the proton. In 1911, Rutherford devised an experiment using this new form of energy: He made a very thin gold foil, much thinner than today's aluminum foil, and let the alpha particles pass through it. What do you think happened?

Rutherford could do both experimental physics and theoretical physics and, using the plum pudding model of the atom, calculated that the alpha particles would experience a deflection of about one degree. Then he did the experiment. To his great surprise, some of the alpha particles were deflected by 90 degrees, and some even came back into the direction from which they came. How could this be?

This is often how physics progresses, precise measurements from careful experiments show how nature behaves, and often it is not what is expected. Now Rutherford was faced with data he could not explain. He knew something was wrong, but what?

The fundamental particles that make up atoms can either have positive electric charge, negative electric charge, or no charge at all. For example, the electrons have negative charge and the protons

(continues on next page)

(continued from previous page)

have positive charge, while the neutrons, having no charge, are neutral. The most important property about charged particles is this: Particles with the same charge repel each other, but particles with opposite charge attract. This means that the positively charged alpha particles are repelled from the positive nucleus of the atoms. Since the charge of both the gold nucleus and the alpha particle was known, Rutherford was able to compute the force between each and from that get the one degree deflection. Rutherford spent many long hours wondering what in the world was wrong but then finally got an idea.

In order to account for the very large deflection he saw in the lab, the force between the alpha particle and the gold nucleus had to be much larger than he had calculated. Rutherford reasoned that a stronger repulsive force would exist if the charge of the nucleus could be squeezed to a much smaller volume. In this case, any incoming alpha particle that got close to the highly concentrated nuclear charge would feel a much stronger force and therefore suffer a much larger deflection. But just how small must the nucleus be to account for the deflections that were measured in the lab? Rutherford calculated that the entire nucleus would have to be stuffed into a region about 100,000 times smaller than the atom. This is so small there is a special unit for it, the fermi. One fermi is one one-hundred thousandths of an angstrom, or 10^{-15} m, also called a femtometer. The electrons must stay at the distance of an angstrom or so, but the positive nucleus would have to be squeezed all the way down to a region of a few fermi. This means the atom is mostly empty space.

This was a major step in modern physics, the discovery of the true nature of an atom in which the nucleus, consisting of protons and neutrons, sits squashed into a tiny volume, while the electrons dance far outside its reach. It did not take long for people to realize that none of the known physics could explain the mysterious rays emitted from the nucleus, nor could it explain anything else about this tiny ball of charge, so small that it makes the tiny atom seem huge by comparison. This is like comparing a football stadium to the entire Earth!

Physics in Europe

Rutherford's picture of the atom, with a tiny nucleus containing neutrons and protons and electrons much further away, threw scientists into a tumultuous sea of debate. Keeping in mind that opposite charges attract, the negative electrons feel an intense attraction to the nucleus, so why didn't the electrons simply fall into the nucleus? No one knew.

One failed attempt was to try to envision the atom as a tiny solar system, with the nucleus being the Sun and the electrons as the planets. The trouble with this model is that as the electrons orbit around the nucleus, they emit radiation. This is a fundamental fact of electromagnetism, that accelerating charges emit radiation. This was well known and, in fact, accounts for how radio towers transmit the energy to your radio. There were two problems: One was that the energy predicted by this was not observed. If that were not bad enough, it also predicted that an atom would collapse in less than a nanosecond, one-billionth of a second. Obviously, this does not happen!

As Wu was working her way through high school in Suchou, the physics world was struggling to understand the fundamental building block of all matter—the atom. Detailed experiments only added to the confusion. To understand the chaos, think about white light. It is known that white light contains all of the colors of the spectrum. To physicists, this means that it contains all of the wavelengths. For example, red light has a wavelength of about 6,800 Å (remember, the angstrom is 10^{-10} m). Green light is about 5,500 Å, and purple is just above 4,000 Å. When one considers the light emitted from the Sun, or any very hot glowing object, energy is radiated at all of these wavelengths and everything in between. This is called a "continuous spectrum." When physicists measured the light coming from hydrogen, the simplest atom, they did not see anything like a continuous spectrum. They discovered that in the visible range, the hydrogen atom emits light at only four wavelengths. Nothing in between, nothing like the continuous spectrum, just four stand-alone wavelengths—four distinct colors. When light contains only specific wavelengths, it is called a "discrete spectrum." The difference between a continuous spectrum and a discrete spectrum is like the difference between a ramp and a staircase.

Physicists were totally baffled: What caused the discrete spectrum? Why were there only four visible colors emitted from hydrogen? Why did classical physics fail? While it is doubtful that Wu was aware of the calamitous state of affairs, there is little doubt she

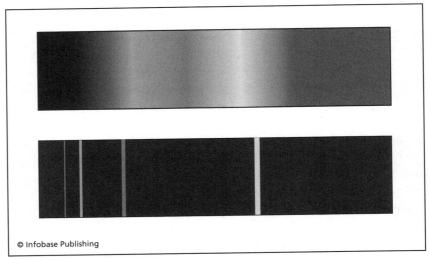

The continuous spectrum (top) versus the discrete, or line, spectrum

wanted to be. She was nurturing a growing interest in science and physics, but her entry into this world would have to wait a while longer. By the time she was about to graduate, European physicists were well on their way to the solution of the problem of the atom.

Quantum Physics, the Early Years

The eventual solution to this conundrum was so strange at the time that some physicists—Albert Einstein, for example—never accepted the "new physics" and took their old notions to the grave. This new view of the world came to be called "quantum mechanics," and all of the previous physics involving gravity and electromagnetism came to be called "classical physics." Quantum mechanics is the physics of the atom and the nucleus, the physics of the microscopic world, the world where the old physics fails. When Wu was "self-learning," she was learning about classical physics, but later, she would help the world understand more about quantum mechanics.

Quantum mechanics is more bizarre than a pride of lions flying through an orange sky. It destroyed the previous concepts of what could be learned and left scientists in a world that is doomed to be limited in what can be known. In classical physics, from a theoretical point of view, things that are observed can be measured exactly (physicists call things that are observed "observables," such as position, energy, or momentum). With quantum mechanics, the value of observables cannot be determined exactly; there is always an uncertainty. In other words, it cannot be determined exactly what will happen: Nature injects an inherent probability to how things behave. Here is an example.

Suppose an electron travels due north toward a solid target with a small hole in it. What happens? According to classical physics, either the electron is stopped by the target or passes straight through, still headed north, if it passes through the hole. This is like shooting a bullet toward a thick steel plate with a one-inch hole. However, according to quantum mechanics, it cannot be determined what the electron will do. If it is aimed directly at the hole, it may be reflected back, or it may pass through, but it will not always be traveling due north. The best quantum mechanics can do is to predict the probability of where it will go, but it can go practically anywhere. This is because classical physics fails on the tiny scale of the atom, where quantum rules.

This fascinating new world is called "nondeterministic" because it cannot be precisely determined what will happen, or where a particle will go, or what an atom will do. Another, perhaps even more important, point about quantum mechanics is that it predicts energy levels are "quantized." In the stair analogy, this is saying that a person can be on the first stair, second, or third, and so on, but never in between. When an atom jumps from one level, which is called a "quantum state," to another level, it emits energy at precisely the difference in energy between the two states. If this is light energy, this means that the light is emitted at precisely one wavelength. If the atom jumps between two other states, light will be emitted at another wavelength, there will be no radiation in between. This is exactly what was observed with hydrogen, and the mystery of the four distinct lines was finally solved. The light that is emitted comes in photons, tiny bundles of energy that carry the precise energy of the difference in the energy levels. When many photons act together it is called a "wave," and that is the wavelength mentioned above.

In order to describe the energy coming from atoms and nuclei, a special unit is used, the electron volt, or eV, for short. When atoms emit visible light, they emit photons that have an energy of about 2 eV. Atoms that have many electrons can sometimes produce higher energy: If the inner electrons, those closest to the nucleus, are ripped free, then the outer electrons cascade down into the open energy level. This can produce energies of 1,000 eV or more, which is called keV (these are rays that people are exposed to when they visit a dentist). As physicists soon learned, the nucleus emits even higher energy, of the order of millions of eV, or MeV.

Although recent experiments represented a great advance in physics, they also brought new worries. Physics often progresses in this manner. When telescopes were invented and people saw Saturn's rings, this was a great discovery, but scientists could not explain what the rings were made of. It would take centuries until people understood that the rings were not great solid pieces, but millions of rock and boulder-sized objects orbiting the magnificent planet. When Rutherford discovered atomic structure, it took almost 20 years to understand it. And so, now another problem cropped up.

The problem has to do with the radiation coming from uranium and other atoms. By now it was known that beta rays were actually electrons. Consider the element cobalt. It is a metal, and like most metals, it is lustrous and silver gray. The nucleus contains 27 protons and 32 neutrons, and as is true for all atoms, the number of electrons is equal to the number of protons. The symbol for cobalt is Co, often written as ^{59}Co. (The 59 indicates the number of neutrons plus protons that reside in the nucleus.) Most atoms have "cousins," or isotopes, that have the same number of protons and electrons but a different number of neutrons. For example, an isotope of cobalt is ^{60}Co (cobalt-60), which has one extra neutron in the nucleus. Chien-shiung Wu would later rock the world when she performed experiments with ^{60}Co, but this part of the story will have to wait.

^{60}Co is not a stable atom; it is radioactive. This means it changes into something else. Another famous example of radioactivity is ^{235}U, uranium-235, which is used in the atomic bomb. An important property of radioactive materials is their half-life, which can be described as follows. Suppose there are 1,000 atoms of ^{235}U, and one waits about 700 million years. After this stretch of time, there would only be about 500 ^{235}U atoms left. It is as if the uranium "decays" with time. In fact, this is precisely how half-life is defined, and for ^{235}U, the half-life is about 700 million years. At the atomic level, however, the word *decay* is not at all appropriate—rather, the nucleus explodes like TNT, releasing a precious store of energy as it changes to another atom or atoms.

While uranium can decay in many different ways, ^{60}Co is more consistent: The form of radioactivity is beta rays and gamma rays. This means that this nucleus, every once in a while, shoots out an electron, along with a gamma particle (photon). The half-life of ^{60}Co is about 5.3 years and it is used today in hospitals around the world to treat cancer patients.

A Profound Mystery

As Wu was toiling at the Suchou school for girls, physicists a continent away were working in their labs, measuring beta decay from various nuclei. They were befuddled by the problem of energy. One of the elements they examined was an isotope of bismuth, ^{210}Bi, known then as radium E. The fact that it underwent beta decay was no great surprise, but the energy of the electrons was surprising. The fastest electron had an energy of about one MeV, but often much slower, less energetic electrons would emerge. In fact, electrons with a whole range of energies, from 0 to 1 MeV, were emitted. The trouble was that after the beta decay, the bismuth atom changed into a polonium atom, and all of the newly formed polonium atoms were exactly the same. So, where did the energy go? Suppose, in one case, an electron zooms out with an energy of 1.0 MeV, and compare that to the case that an electron was emitted with an energy 0.5 MeV. Where did the other 0.5 MeV go? No one knew. All the while Wu was in school in China, physicists, mostly in England and Germany, tried to solve this puzzle.

Rutherford suggested that all of the electrons are actually ejected with the same energy, but some of them lose it to its surroundings, bouncing into other atoms on the way out of the material. This is like having a race where a crowd of people huddle right in the middle of the track. One or two runners might make it through without collisions, but most would bump into somebody. Even though most of the competitors can run at about the same speed, there will be a wide range of speeds as the runners emerge from the crowd.

Niels Bohr (1885–1962), one of the fathers of quantum mechanics, came to suspect that energy was not conserved. Conservation of energy is one of the bedrock assumptions in physics. It is, perhaps, not so much an assumption as an empirical law that has never been found to be violated. It is like saying all humans breathe. No one has checked every human on Earth, but surely this is believed to be true, and if someone asserts to find an island of people who do not breathe, this claim would be found suspect. Bohr's speculation was met with the same suspicion, yet it was the only explanation. While Wu was learning about conservation of energy, European physicists were doing experiments where it was not the case. Or, was it?

The physicists were using a device called a spectrometer, an instrument used even more widely today. A spectrometer measures the speed, and therefore the energy, of charge particles. It consists of a magnetic field and particle detectors. The key to its operation is due

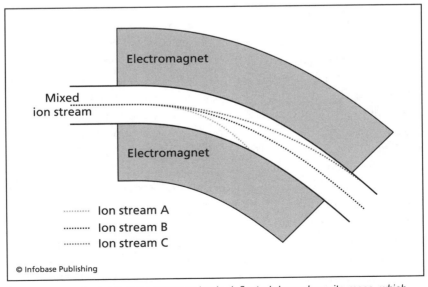

In a mass spectrometer, the amount an ion is deflected depends on its mass, which enables scientists to determine its mass

to the magnetic field that exerts a sideways force on charged particles. For example, suppose Ping-Pong balls are thrown due north, but there is a wind coming from due west. The balls will be deflected to the side, where they hit a wall. The faster the ball is tossed, the further it will go before it hits the wall. In fact, its speed can be determined by measuring where it hits the wall. In a spectrometer, the magnetic field takes the place of the wind, and detectors are placed along the wall, allowing scientists to measure where the electron hit.

By the time James Chadwick (1891–1974), English physicist and Nobel Prize winner for his discovery of the neutron, performed his experiments, it was already known that the other kinds of decays— the alpha particles (helium nuclei consisting of two protons and two neutrons) and gamma rays (photons)—were emitted with a certain, unchanging energy. This would make even more sense when quantum mechanics was developed, pointing to discrete energy levels. But Chadwick found a continuous spectrum for the electrons, meaning that they could have a wide range of energies, which in turn indicated that a lot of energy was mysteriously disappearing.

Actually, it was worse than that. One of the most important kinds of principles in physics are conservation laws. Conservation of charge was never violated, and conservation of energy was also believed to hold true, and although some questioned it, most were looking for another explanation of the behavior of beta decay. Another cherished conservation law concerns angular momentum. For a system where no outside forces act, then angular momentum cannot change: This is the law of conservation of angular momentum, which includes spin, the intrinsic angular momentum that elementary particles have. Physicists could measure the angular momentum of the original nucleus and the final nucleus and also knew the electron carried away exactly one-half unit of spin. This led to the conclusion that the angular momentum changed by half a unit, when it should not change at all.

Looking back, this double whammy, as might be said today, could have helped solve the riddle. Any physicist could take a little bad medicine, but no one could swallow the notion that both conservation of energy and conservation of angular momentum were violated. There had to be a better explanation.

Two of the great physicists at that time were Wolfgang Pauli (1900–58), a German, and Enrico Fermi (1901–54), an Italian. Pauli suggested that another particle, so far undetected, was created in beta decay. To understand his idea, the process of beta decay should be examined a little more carefully. First of all, where does the electron emitted in beta decay come from? It was correctly believed that it was not one of the electrons surrounding the nucleus; this number remains the same in ^{60}Co decay. Plus, it could have energies that far exceed the energy of the outer electrons. Thus, it must come from the nucleus. But, the nucleus contained only protons and neutrons, and no electrons were ever measured to be in the nucleus. So, where did the electron come from? The answer must be that it is created, and as soon as it is, it is ejected from the nucleus. Pauli suggested that another particle was also created at this time, and it must be neutral in order not to violate conservation of charge. It would be like the neutron, he suggested, only smaller (meaning lighter). Fermi

Wu with theoretical physicist and friend Wolfgang Pauli (AIP Emilio Segrè Visual Archives, Segrè Collection)

called this hypothetical particle a "small neutron," which in Italian is the *neutrino.*

The neutrino would have to be a very strange particle, nothing like any that had been known. In 1927, in a crucial experiment, C. D. Ellis and W. A. Wooster, coworkers of Chadwick at the Cavendish Laboratory, surrounded the radioactive material in a calorimeter, an instrument that measures the total energy by measuring the rise in temperature. The calorimeter was constructed so that all of the electrons would be trapped. If all of the electrons had the same energy, it was expected that the instrument should measure a temperature rise corresponding to about 1 MeV per electron. In fact, though, they measured an energy of only about one-third of that. If, like undetected spies stealing secrets, this energy was secretly carried away by neutrinos, they would have to be very undetectable indeed—not one of them was stopped in a calorimeter big enough to stop every electron.

This is a typical example of how physics progresses. Although sometimes discoveries are made by doing careful experiments, other times predictions are made that are based on the principles that are known. The neutrino would be detected, but it would take another 20 years, long after Wu had left China.

The Nuclear World

2

By 1900, the dynasty system in China was about to end. Perhaps the reforms it brought to China were responsible for its own demise, but one of those reforms was public education. Although in the early years of the 20th century, the number of public schools bloomed throughout this vast land, there was one proviso that may seem strange today—no girls were allowed. The official end of the dynasties came with the Revolution of 1911. In this year, China became a republic. This was nothing like the American Revolution, and after it ended, it was not even clear who was in charge of the country. Although Yüan Shih-k'ai (Yuan Shikai; 1859–1916) was elected as the first president of this fledgling republic, there was little central rule, and different parts of China had different laws, many areas being ruled by warlords. It was in this confusion that

Wu Chung-i was able to establish his little school, the school that started Wu Chien-shiung on her historic path that would bring her to the United States.

Courageous Hero

By the time the United States was enjoying the Roaring Twenties, China was still struggling with its new form of government. There were attempts to return to the dynasties of old, and a feeling of resentment toward the influence of Japan was growing. Japan had issued the famous list of Twenty-one Demands that would have practically reduced China to a protectorate of Japan. In response, there was a wave of nationalism sweeping through parts of China, especially among students.

One of these students was a girl whose name translates into English as "Courageous Hero." She led hundreds of student protesters through the streets of Nanking in the early 1930s. The goal was to reach the presidential mansion, so Courageous Hero had to navigate her flock through the backstreets so as not to be stopped. When the group reached the mansion, they held what today would be called a "sit-in," waiting resolutely until their voices would be heard. Finally, with snow sweeping down from the midnight sky, General Chiang Kai-shek (Jiang Jieshi) came out, listened to Courageous Hero, and promised to do what he could. The father of Courageous Hero gave her this name because that is what he hoped she would be. And, that she was. Not so much in the tough world of politics but in the tougher world of science. In Chinese, Courageous Hero is Chien-shiung.

In the summer after Wu graduated—at the top of her class—from the girls school in Suchou, a letter came bearing good news: She was accepted at the prestigious National Central University in Nanking. She would go, but she expected to major in education, even though she confided in her father the desire to study physics. Her father was not the kind of man to let the young girl down, so he went out and got advanced books on physics and mathematics. She was accustomed to self-learning and spent the summer preparing for the university.

X-rays and Early Research

Wu graduated from the National Central University in 1934 and became a teacher in a small university, but she wanted to learn more physics. Within a year, she obtained a research position at the National Academy of Sciences in Shanghai in the field of X-ray crystallography. X-rays are a form of electromagnetic radiation, like light, but with a wavelength of only a few angstroms, which is also the typical distance between atoms in a solid. Due to the fact that the wavelength is about the same as the atomic spacing, there is a strong interaction between the radiation and the solid. Now, there are two kinds of solid materials: amorphous and crystal. In an amorphous substance, the atoms or molecules are arranged randomly. Like people packed in a large party, there is no order. Crystal materials are like the seats in a movie theater, where people are arranged neatly in rows and columns. When X-rays propagate through the ordered rows and columns of a crystal lattice, the strong interaction mentioned above leaves a distinct pattern in the emerging X-ray beam, what physicists call a "diffraction pattern." For an amorphous material, the random nature of the atoms washes out any pattern, but for crystals, the pattern can be read as easily as a signature. This is exactly what Wu was doing just after she graduated from college.

In the English language the word *crystal* can be deceiving. What is called crystal glass is not a crystal at all: Glass is amorphous. On the other hand, all metals are crystalline, where the atoms fall obediently in line, making distinct rows and columns. However, different materials have different atomic spacing, and furthermore, they form different kinds of crystal shapes. For these reasons, no two different materials have the same structure, and therefore, no two different materials have the same diffraction pattern.

By making careful measurements of the diffraction patterns and understanding the physics involved, Wu began her career as an experimental physicist. The techniques are used today and represent one of the ways we have to determine the complex compositions of the myriad materials that are tested in labs throughout the world.

Wu wanted to learn more physics, but there were no graduate schools in physics in China. The person from whom Wu was learning this new field had received her Ph.D. from the University of Michigan, halfway around the world. With the help of her uncle, Wu was able to come up with the money she needed and left her family and China in 1936 by boat, heading for the state of Michigan. Her plans were to obtain a Ph.D. and immediately return to China in order to help the country that gave her such a good start in life. But, her plans would change far more than she could ever dream.

Wu wearing her pearl necklace (AIP Emilio Segrè Visual Archives, Physics Today Collection)

Wu Arrives in the United States

Wu's first stop in the United States on her way to Michigan was San Francisco, California, so close to the University of California at Berkeley that she decided to visit the campus. Her ship landed at the end of the summer of 1936, and she luckily had time before classes at Michigan began. And, there, on the Berkeley campus, a curious connection between Wu's past and future life was formed. The grandson of former (and first) Chinese president Yüan Shih-k'ai, Yüan Chia-liu (Yuan Jialiu), was studying physics at Berkeley, and six years after Wu's arrival, they would be married. But, that is not the only thing she liked about Berkeley.

In some respects, the timing of Wu's arrival in the United States could not have been better, as the United States had decided to beef up its program in physics. Much of the current physics when Wu was in China was performed in Europe, but the United States wanted that to change. Rutherford himself helped this metamorphosis occur. He had been working with radioactive nuclei for years, and was even able to transform oxygen to nitrogen by bombarding oxygen with alpha particles, but he soon exhausted much of what could be done with the natural resources he had at hand. In 1927, he urged physicists to develop higher energy and more abundant sources of particles to probe the enigmatic world of nuclear physics.

The strengthening of U.S. physics programs continued in the East; there were renowned physics departments at the University of Chicago, Harvard, Johns Hopkins, Michigan, and Princeton. Then, the administrators of the California Polytechnic Institute and Berkeley started talking about establishing physics in California. And, as the saying goes, they put their money where their mouth was. With this new funding, they were able to hire top physicists and provide equipment for experimentalists.

The Cyclotron and the Beginning of Nuclear Physics

It was at this time that the noted nuclear physicist and experimentalist Ernest Lawrence (1901–58) had an idea. Responding to Rutherford's call for high-energy sources, Lawrence conceived of the idea of what is now called a "cyclotron." It was known that charged particles could be accelerated in an electric field, but to get really fast moving particles—particles with a lot of energy—it would take a long distance. This is why airport runways are so long: It takes a long time, and therefore a long distance, to get the jet to high enough speeds for takeoff. Particles must be accelerated in a vacuum; otherwise they will continually hit into other particles and never gain much energy. But, it is difficult, and expensive, to make a mile-long linear accelerator (linacs). Lawrence had a better idea.

From the discussion about the spectrometer, it was learned that a magnetic field exerts a sideways force on a charged particle that is moving through it. In fact, this will cause the particle to travel in a circle with constant speed. If an electric field is applied perpendicular to the magnetic field, this will make the particle speed up, just as they do in the linacs. But, since the magnetic field is present, the particle will still try to go in a circle. The combined effect of both fields will cause the particle to spiral out, gaining speed as it does so. The trouble is, as soon as it goes halfway around, the particle will be

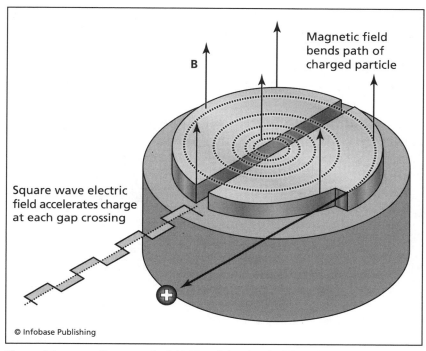

B

Magnetic field bends path of charged particle

Square wave electric field accelerates charge at each gap crossing

© Infobase Publishing

The cyclotron uses the magnetic field (B) and the electric field to accelerate charged particles, which spiral out as shown by the spinal path.

going in the opposite direction of the electric field that made it speed up, which will slow it back down. Lawrence had the idea to switch the polarity of the electric field at precisely the time the particle goes halfway around. This changes the direction of the electric field so that it continues to speed up the particle. By repeatedly switching the electric field in this way, the particle will continuously speed up. This was just a theory, though. The question remained if it could be built and would work.

It worked. In 1931, Lawrence and his graduate student M. Stanley Livingston built the cyclotron and were able to accelerate protons to an energy of 1.1 MeV. This was truly the beginning of the next era of nuclear physics.

By the time Wu arrived at Berkeley in 1936, it had become a hubbub of activity among nuclear physicists. It was a great opportunity for Wu, seeing a world-class university in an exciting new field. She called it "the top of the world" for anyone interested in nuclear physics. But, what about the University of Michigan, her original school of choice?

Michigan already had 600 Chinese students—that is partly how she made her connection there. Wu had struggled all her life to learn physics, and this goal was much more important to her than being able to fit in, like a piece in a jigsaw puzzle. In her pursuit to learn physics, Wu also had to fight against the imbalanced educational system that favored males over females. At the University of Michigan, women were not allowed in the student union, and this rule must have raked against her sense of education, brought up by a father who fought to bring education to women and treat them as equal to men.

So, Wu accepted an offer at Berkeley and entered the new epicenter of nuclear physics. It is helpful to understand how important the cyclotron was to physics, and indirectly, to Wu. The world of nuclear physics was embryonic; only a handful of experiments had been performed. The reason experiments are so hard to perform is not simply because the nuclei are so small but they are all positively charged. Since like charges repel, whenever one nucleus gets near another nucleus, they fly away from each other, never even getting the chance to truly interact. With the cyclotron, physicists were able to obtain particles that were traveling so fast they would overcome this barrier of repulsion. For the first time, controlled nuclear reactions were possible.

Lawrence headed the physics department at Berkeley and worked with the brilliant Emilio Segrè (1905–89). Wu might have been worried about working with a man known to have a fiery temper, but Courageous Hero fit right into his research team. Segrè always expected her to excel and treated her "like family."

Although many people had trouble pronouncing her given name and instead called her Miss Wu, later Madame Wu, Chien-shiung did not take on an Americanized name, as many Asians do. She also continued to wear traditional Chinese clothing, a habit she would maintain all her life. There was one other tradition she could not give up, a tradition that was perhaps reinforced after her first meal in the Berkeley cafeteria. Wu immediately began looking for places that served Chinese food. At a local bakery, she met Ursula Schaefer, a German graduate student who shared Wu's dislike of cafeteria food. They quickly became friends and also found a way to eat Chinese food for 25 cents, a bargain even then. They got to know a Chinese caterer not far from the university that would let them eat banquet leftovers. Wu and Schaefer would be friends for the rest of their lives and were willing to speak openly to each other, not only of things they agreed on but of things they disagreed about.

For her doctoral research, Wu began looking at the X-rays associated with beta decay and devised experimental methods to distinguish different energies of this radiation. In her collaborations with Segrè, they were able to document the complete chain of radioactivity for different elements. This means that they were able to identify every nucleus that was created from the fission and each element that was formed after that. Although this information would soon be used by Los Alamos National Laboratory, it was not published until after the end of World War II.

Wu was able to obtain her Ph.D. in four years, in spite of the terrible news of 1939: Japan invaded China. Two years later, Japan would surprise the United States with its attack on Pearl Harbor, but the invasion of China had been expected. With this event, Wu was cut off from her family, whom she would never see again. She resolved to work harder than ever, and after the completion of her Ph.D. in 1940, she was asked to stay on at Berkeley to continue her research. Segrè thought that the university should hire her as a regular faculty member, but this was still in the days when women in science were not considered suitable for faculty.

Ask Miss Wu

Shortly after the completion of her Ph.D. occurred the famous "Ask Miss Wu" episode. To understand the significance of this, one should take a slight detour into the rage in physics at the time. Two years earlier, another woman, Lise Meitner (1878–1968) from Sweden, and Otto Frisch (1904–79), her nephew, made sense of the puzzling data of a Berlin laboratory by assuming that certain nuclei split apart, a process Meitner called "fission."

Fission instantly captured the attention of physicists and soon would capture the attention of the entire world. There are two battles continuously raging inside the tiny nucleus. In the case of uranium and many other heavy elements, the army of protons strongly repel each other and are always seeking ways to secede from the tiny kingdom. The nuclear force is the peacekeeper, exerting an attractive force on both the neutrons and protons. For small atoms, such as helium and nitrogen, the nucleus is stable, but for atoms bigger than iron, the nucleus can undergo fission and give off energy while doing so.

This tiny pocket of energy is nature's gift, or curse, to humans. When used for good, it can provide power to sustain our life long after the oil fields have been depleted. When used in weapons, such as atomic bombs, it can destroy life in milliseconds and turn the planet into a radioactive wasteland. This vast energy source was not lost on the physicists of the time, and the cyclotron at Berkeley was the perfect instrument to study how a nucleus splits apart.

By 1940, Britain, Germany, France, and the United States were working on fission. It was known that there are two kinds of fission: spontaneous fission and induced fission. The first kind is responsible for part of the (very low) natural background radiation and results when a nucleus splits apart with no help from outside forces. Induced fission occurs when the nucleus gets a helping hand, often in the form of a neutron. The uranium nucleus is like an overfilled balloon. It can suddenly and with no warning "spontaneously" burst, or it can be "induced" to burst, if someone sticks it with a pin, for example.

When a uranium nucleus undergoes fission, one of the by-products is a pair of neutrons. These neutrons can induce two more nuclei to split, and they will contribute a total of four neutrons. They, in turn, can induce four more nuclei to split, and this creates eight, and then 16, and so on. This process is a chain reaction, and physicists calculated that 60 kilograms of uranium could release as much energy as about 15,000 tons—30 million pounds—of TNT, in milliseconds. Hiroshima, in Japan, witnessed the grim truth of the estimate on August 6, 1945, when "Little Boy," the code name of the first atomic bomb ever used in warfare, was detonated at an altitude of 1,900 feet (580 m).

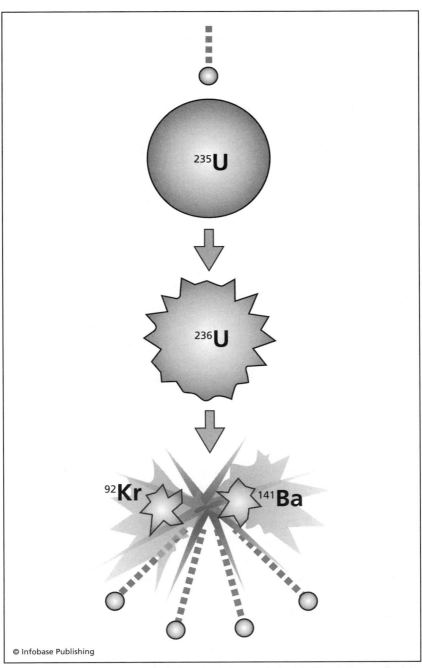

A uranium nucleus is hit by a neutron (top), which causes fission. The nucleus splits into other elements, plus it releases three more neutrons, which will cause more fission.

Uranium is not the only fissionable material; another is pluto-nium. Unlike uranium, however, plutonium cannot be dug out of the earth. Plutonium is made in the laboratory. It is the so-called dream come true for the age-old alchemists who tried so hard to change lead into gold. But, to make plutonium, physicists did not use potions and chants read from some obscure book of spells; they used the cyclotron.

While uranium has 92 protons in the nucleus, plutonium has 94. At Berkeley, Lawrence and others were able to create plutonium by bombarding uranium with deuterons, particles that contain one pro-ton and one neutron. It is a long and tedious process, but the prize was a highly fissionable material, a material that was believed would create a chain reaction.

The person trying to make that chain reaction work was Fermi. In 1940, he was in charge of the reactor built in Hanford, Washington, but he was in trouble. All the calculations aside, the chain reaction did not sustain itself, fizzling out in a few hours. He suspected some fission by-product was gumming up the works, but no one really knew what was wrong. As the story goes, someone told him to "Ask Miss Wu." And, he did.

Wu had just received her Ph.D. and was right in the middle of the activity of nuclear physics at Berkeley. Robert Oppenheimer (1904–67), one of the most brilliant theoretical physicists, called her "the authority" in nuclear matters due to her intricate knowledge of the field. Word of Wu's mastery of this complex field spread throughout the nation, and when Fermi was stuck with his fizzling reactions, he turned to Miss Wu.

During the fission of plutonium, as is true for the fission of any heavy nucleus, many by-products, or daughter products, as they are called, can be produced. Wu realized that during the fission of plutonium, ^{137}Xe (xenon-137) was being produced and collected in the reaction chamber. Xenon is a heavy noble gas and, like all noble gases, does not react chemically with other materials very much. The isotope ^{137}Xe happens to be very receptive of neutrons and eats them up like a frog catching flies. This explains why the fission process ended. As the xenon built up, more and more neutrons were cap-tured by the otherwise inert gas, and soon there were not enough left to trigger the induced fission that Fermi was trying to achieve.

The only way to overcome this problem was to put more plutonium in the reactor, but was there room? The physicists had calculated how much plutonium was needed and specified room for that much, and no more. Of course, they had no idea at that time about the xenon problem. As the story goes, with the Wu diagnosis, the problem was solved due to the foresight of an engineer known as "Uncle George," who made the core bigger than what the physicists' designs called for. He said, "I don't care what those long-hairs say, add ten percent more core to the pile." With this, there was more room for the extra plutonium.

Wu's hard work was now paying off. With her correct diagnosis of the xenon problem and the best physicists in the country singing her praise, Wu was ready to strike out on her own path. She was ready to carve out her niche as one of the best experimental physicists in the country.

The Manhattan Project

3

After having had to overcome prejudice against women in her native country, Wu now faced it in her new country. As she became an expert in nuclear physics, it was clear that she belonged in a university environment, but many top universities did not think women should be hired as faculty members. As World War II raged, it became clear that the expertise of such a fine physicist could not be wasted, and it was not long before Wu was making contributions to the war effort. Wu overcame these prejudices and contributed to the biggest, most secret project ever devised by the United States.

Overcoming Prejudice

Wu was living two lives. One was that of the rewarding and success-ful hardworking physicist whose excellent reputation was spreading fast. The other was as the Chinese immigrant who was worried about her family in her homeland under Japanese occupation and meanwhile saw anti-Asian sentiments explode after Japan attacked the United States on December 7, 1941, at Pearl Harbor.

In the wake of Pearl Harbor, Japanese nationals and Japanese Americans in the United States were forcibly sent into internment camps. Some people did not differentiate between Chinese and Japanese, even though the Chinese, including Wu's father, Chung-i, were bravely fighting against the Japanese to defend their land. Under these circumstances, life was not any easier for Wu, who was still importing fabrics from Taiwan and China that she used to make her traditional Chinese dress. Two Japanese students at Berkeley gave her flowers, trying to make the best of a tense situation.

This prejudice, as well as growing xenophobia (fear of foreigners), affected Wu's professional life as strongly as it affected her personal life. Rumors that Germany was working on an atomic bomb were substantiated, and Adolf Hitler's terrible program to eradicate the Jews was under way. This caused a number of Jewish physicists to flee Germany, including Leo Szilard (1898–1964), who came to the United States. Szilard is credited with being the first person who actually predicted the possibility of a nuclear chain reaction. He understood the deadly consequences of such a powerful weapon and looked for ways to keep it secret. He applied for a patent on the plans for the atomic bomb in 1934. He wanted to give the patent to the British War Office so it could be classified and kept secret, but the office rejected it.

Another German physicist who fled his home country to go to the United States was Albert Einstein (1879–1955). His special theory of relativity was a groundbreaking development in 1905, and his general theory of relativity was even more revolutionary, making him one of the most respected physicists in the world. Szilard, along with Eugene Wigner (1902–95) and Edward Teller (1908–2003) two excellent physicists, persuaded Einstein to write President Franklin D. Roosevelt a letter admonishing the United States to get more deeply involved in making the bomb.

Whereas very few letters written to the president are read by the president, one coming from Einstein had a much better chance than most. Alexander Sachs, a Lithuanian-born economist and adviser to Roosevelt, persuaded him to believe what Einstein stated in the letter. The president was indeed convinced, and in response, in 1940, the covert Manhattan Project began, starting with a $40,000 grant to Columbia University in New York City. Although that is not enough to cover the expenses of a graduate student in physics today, it was enough to start what might be called the most important project the United States has ever initiated. At about this time, Oppenheimer had gone to Los Alamos, New Mexico, to design and build the first atomic bomb. Many of the Berkeley graduate students were invited to join the project, but not Wu because she was Chinese.

Wu not only was an expert on fission but also had a detailed knowledge of nuclear physics few other people in the world had. Consequently, during her time as a researcher at Berkeley, she was invited to many universities to give talks about her research. Although her Ph.D. thesis, entitled "I. The Internal and External Continuous X-Rays Excited by the Beta-Particles of PHOSPHOROUS-32. II. Some Fission Products of Uranium," described the ways in which particles lose energy as they travel through materials, emitting X-rays, the explosive area of nuclear physicists reached out to her and thus began a lifelong involvement with this fascinating field of physics. She began to study how nuclei decay and what other nuclei they decay into. At this time, this information was worth more than gold.

From her childhood days in Liu Ho to her college days in Nanking, Wu was always interested in physics, yearning to understand the natural world around her. Comfortable working in a laboratory, she was finally in her element. Wu was performing careful experiments that had never been done before, discovering things no one knew before. Describing the decay of the noble gases and measuring all of the nuclei formed in the decay chain were new and important tasks needed by the nuclear physics community.

As she traveled throughout the country in 1941 giving talks about her research, she continued to wear traditional Chinese dress. She was very beautiful and charming, and a California newspaper reporter said she looked, "as though she might be an actress or an artist or a daughter of wealth in search of Occidental culture."

Although Wu learned English before she arrived at Berkeley, she never quite mastered the language. There were times when her pronunciation was so bad she could not be understood, and during times of excitement, her grammar would nosedive. Articles were the first casualties, being left out altogether, and then verbs joined the ranks of the missing. Wu set out to overcome this obstacle with her usual meticulousness. She would carefully write out her talks beforehand, rehearse them, and follow her notes during the lecture.

More Research on X-rays

At the time, very little was known about radioactivity, and physicists were desperate to compare theory to experiment in order to understand the complex workings of the tiny nucleus. One problem concerned the two kinds of beta radioactivity. Beta radiation simply means electrons are being emitted from the nuclei. In some radioactive substances, beta radiation was accompanied by weak gamma radiation. Gamma radiation is the emission of photons, and in this process, the photons could have any energy.

Theorists suspected two possible mechanisms for this weak gamma radiation. One was that after the electron was emitted, the resulting change in the nucleus caused a photon to be emitted. These are called internal X-rays. The other possibility was that when an electron got too close to the nucleus, the intense interaction caused photons to be emitted, which were called external X-rays. But, which, if either, was right? Wu decided to find out.

Wu was able to find errors in other experiments that had large discrepancies between the experimental result and the theory. For example, in a 1941 article in *Physical Review* she wrote: "The large discrepancies between their experimental results and theoretical calculation may be explained by the fact that part of the external x-rays excited on the [magnetic] pole faces and walls has gotten into the counter." She was able to conclude that the proportion of internal to external X-rays stood at one to four and thereby solved the vexatious problem of weak gamma rays. Wu was making her reputation by these kinds of very accurate experiments. She was able to figure out what was important in the experiments and what would lead to errors.

With a Ph.D. in physics in hand, what kinds of jobs could Wu look for? With World War II under way, many physicists got jobs working for the Department of Defense or for companies contracted by the department. This door, however, was closed to Wu due to her nationality. And, at that time, there was hardly any commercial interest in nuclear physicists. Besides, Wu wanted to continue her research. The perfect solution would have been a university position as a faculty member in the physics department. This would give her the opportunity to continue her research and teach her knowledge to young people in a new world in which the comprehension of nuclear physics was essential.

Although Wu was ready to strike out on her own by 1942, she was battling not only prejudice against Asians but also prejudice against women. Many men still held the archaic notion that women belonged in the home, belief even shared by many well-educated university professors. This made Wu's search for a university position very difficult, but not impossible. Wu's situation was further complicated by her recent marriage to Yuan, whom she had met upon arrival to Berkeley. (In the United States he rendered his name as Luke Chia-liu Yuan.) So, instead of just one post, they both were looking for a place where two physicists could work.

The Move East

One of the new technologies at this time was radar, a device that emits radio waves and uses the reflected radiation to find incoming airplanes. Common today, as many motorists belatedly realize after being ticketed for speeding, this was a new technology back then, and physicists were badly needed to build and design radar systems. Yuan got a job working for RCA Laboratories in Princeton, New Jersey, so he and Wu moved to the East.

Wu then got a position at Smith College, in Northampton, Massachusetts. She and Yuan met midway in New York on the weekends. The appointment at Smith was not the ideal position she was looking for. In colleges, faculty members often spend most of their time teaching. This highlights a difference between colleges and universities that still holds true today. Many colleges are essentially teaching institutions, where dedicated faculty members spend most of their time teaching. Research is important, too, but secondary. In research institutions, it is the other way around, where the professors spend most of their time doing research, often getting external funding agencies to finance their research through grants. Although Wu liked teaching, she felt an instinctive need to be in a laboratory, from morning until night if she had her way.

Then some good news came her way at a conference in Boston. She met up with Lawrence, who knew her very well from her time at Berkeley, and confided to him that she was not happy being deprived of laboratory work. Lawrence did not waste time in spreading the word that an exceptionally talented physicist was looking for a research faculty position. In no time, Wu had offers from Princeton, Berkeley, and other institutions, but her choice was easy. In order to be with Yuan, she accepted the offer from Princeton University.

In this photo, taken at Smith College in 1942, Wu is assembling an electrostatic generator. (AIP Emilio Segrè Visual Archives)

The circumstances there, however, were puzzling to Wu. She had been hired to teach at Princeton, where female students were not admitted at that time! There was a severe shortage of physicists in this field, and this dearth of university professors, coupled with Wu's ability, got her the job. Nevertheless, one of the oddities that Wu noticed about her new country was the inequality between men and women. In the midst of the ideal of American equality was the discriminatory policy that some of the best universities did not accept female students.

Wu was delighted to go to a major research institution but she was still involved in teaching. Naval officers were being sent there to further their knowledge of engineering, which has physics as the foundational science. At Princeton, Wu was able to help them. She said: "They were good students, but they were afraid of physics, and first you had to get them over the fear." Although Wu is most renowned for her research, this quote provides an insight into her feelings about teaching, showing that she also took this part of her career seriously.

The "Blackboard Interviews"

Harold Urey had studied under Gilbert Lewis at Berkeley and in 1942, was at Columbia University devising ways to enrich uranium. After only a few months at Princeton, Wu went to an interview at Columbia. The research was classified, and the two men who interviewed Wu were careful not to talk about the details of their ongoing research. But, by the end of the two-day interview, Wu already knew what it was all about. How did she find out?

The language of physics is mathematics, and when two physicists discuss a problem, they usually end up at a blackboard, scribbling the equations that are the nouns and verbs of their language. Wu had been in several labs and many rooms and could read the blackboards as easily as you can read this text. They all laughed at their misguided attempt at secrecy and offered Wu a position. She accepted, and in 1944, under the Division of War Research at Columbia, Wu officially began work on the Manhattan Project.

The research that Wu inferred from reading the blackboards had to do with the enrichment of uranium used to make the atomic bomb. Uranium comes in different isotopes, the most abundant being ^{238}U (uranium-238), which has 146 neutrons and 92 protons. But, this is a rather stable nucleus and is not useful for fission. The fissionable material is ^{235}U. With three fewer neutrons, the nucleus is much more likely to explode and is the form of uranium needed to make a chain reaction. However, only a little less than 1 percent of uranium found in nature is the fissionable kind.

Wu was offered the position at Columbia to help "enrich" uranium, that is, obtain ^{235}U from ^{238}U. The enrichment technique they used was called the "gaseous diffusion process." The first step, after having pure, or nearly pure, uranium, is to make it into a gas. The best way to do this is to mix it with fluorine: One uranium atom and six fluorine atoms make uranium hexafluoride, UF_6, or uranium hex, as they called it.

This is a quite unpleasant substance, toxic and corrosive to most metals, and it is highly reactive with water. However, it is easy to vaporize. Thus, they were able to create a gas of $^{238}UF_6$, with a little bit of $^{235}UF_6$. Wu's job was to capture the $^{235}UF_6$, from which they could create the prize worth more than solid gold: ^{235}U.

The only difference between these two isotopes of uranium hex is that $^{235}UF_6$ is a little bit lighter. This means that on average, these molecules will be moving a bit faster than the heavier ones. The idea was to place a membrane that would pass the gas from its original chamber to another sealed container. Since the lighter $^{235}UF_6$ molecules move faster, they will bang into the membrane a little more often than the heavier ones so that the second chamber will have a higher ratio of $^{235}UF_6$ to $^{238}UF_6$. This can be repeated over and over again, in a cascade process, until there is very little $^{238}UF_6$ remaining. There are many interesting details about this process—such as how to make those membranes—that were secret and are still classified to this day, but the process worked and was used to obtain nearly pure samples of ^{235}U. This was an extremely important part of the Manhattan Project: Without this success, the atomic bomb might not have been developed by the United States.

The Manhattan Project was more than simply a research project. It was a bold new attempt with grand and lofty ideals to bring together the country's best scientists and engineers to do something that was never done before, something that might have been impossible—build an atomic bomb. It brought together universities, industry, and companies that were capable of building and operating the large plants necessary for the research. Nazi Germany was working on making an atom bomb, and the idea of having such weapons under the control of Hitler was a chilling thought. Hitler was responsible for the murder of millions of Jews, and many other heinous war crimes, and Americans felt it was their duty to obtain this device before Germany did.

One of the most important instruments to be used in connection with radioactive sources is a device to measure the amount of radiation they emit. This is not only important to understand the physics of what is going on during fission but is essential to protect the workers from the potentially harmful effects of radiation. Almost everyone knows the name of this device, the Geiger counter.

Fission versus Fusion

Two of the greatest sources of energy are fission and fusion. As explained earlier in the text, fission is the process by which energy is released when a nucleus splits apart. This is possible for any nucleus bigger than iron. For nuclei smaller than iron, and especially the lightest nuclei such as hydrogen and helium, energy is released in a different but complementary process—fusion. Fusion is the process whereby two small nuclei "fuse" together to make a bigger nucleus. In this process of coming together, energy is released. Fusion will give off energy as long as the end nucleus is no bigger than iron.

It may seem strange that in fission, energy is released when the nucleus splits apart and in fusion, energy is released when they come together. The reason for this is due to the two different forces at work in the nucleus. Fission occurs in the big nuclei where the large number of protons leads to a very large electric repulsion, which overcomes the attractive nuclear force. The energy that is released comes from this stored-up repulsive energy of all of the protons. In fusion, where there are only a few protons, the nuclear attractive force is much greater than the electric repulsive force. When two light nuclei come together in fusion, the energy that is given off is supplied by the very strong, attractive, nuclear force.

One of Wu's contributions during this period was to improve the Geiger counter, which is made from a tube filled with an inert gas, such as helium. Some of the inert gases, also called noble gases, are helium, neon, argon, and one that was already discussed, xenon. When a particle comes flying through the inert gas it can ionize the atoms, which means it rips one or more of the electrons away from the nucleus. Now, for a brief time, the gas has charged particles, the ions and the electrons, and can therefore conduct electricity. This tiny electric current is amplified and can be detected. The amount of radiation is proportional to the amount of current the Geiger counter measures. With Wu's improvements, better and more accurate readings could be made, allowing the physicists to understand better the maturing field of nuclear physics.

The nuclear attractive force is stronger than the electric repulsion only for very short distances, lengths not much greater than the size of a nucleus. In chapter 4, it will be seen how Wu made a contribution in this area: the range of nuclear forces.

Fusion is the most abundant source of energy in the entire universe and occurs at a furious rate in the core of all stars. In the Sun, for example, hydrogen is transformed into helium through fusion, and the energy given off is what nurtures and sustains life on this planet. There have been research programs around the world that try to harness this awesome source of energy, but much progress needs to be made before this process can be used for commercial power sources.

Nuclear plants are scattered across the globe and are expected to increase in number in developing countries. These are fission reactors, where uranium is used and the energy given off is used to boil water and turn it to steam, which can be used to create electricity. The biggest problem with nuclear reactors is the spent fuel, the by-products of fission that are still radioactive and harmful to life, but not useful for obtaining energy. Fusion, on the other hand, is much "cleaner" and represents an important potential source of energy for future generations.

In the approximately 10 years since her arrival in the United States, Wu had already made important contributions in nuclear physics, as well as groundbreaking inroads into university life. But, for Wu, this is only the beginning. One of her former graduate students, Noemie Koller, is currently an experimental nuclear physicist in the Department of Physics and Astronomy at Rutgers University, New Jersey. In a 1997 article in *Physics and Society*, Koller stated: "There has been much progress since Chien-Shiung Wu first landed in California in 1936, both in physics and in the recognition of professional women, much of it due to the perseverance, enlightenment and accomplishment of women like her. We will remember the spirit of dedication to science and to her people that characterized Chien-Shiung Wu."

4

After the War

By the time World War II came to a close, Wu had established herself as a proficient and respected experimental physicist. It was both an exciting and worrisome time in Wu's career. She was pleased with her record and the contributions she had made but was concerned about which new area of research she should probe. The next problem she chose to tackle had to be an important one, yet one she could either solve or one in which she could make a significant contribution. After careful thought, Wu chose an area of research that defined a significant part of her career, and her choice propelled her to international acclaim. Her work on beta decay was historic and took her to the heights of nuclear physics.

Good News

The first piece of good news after the war came from China: Wu's family was well. In fact, her father had engineered the construction of the Burma Road. The road, built by hand, snaked through the tortuous Himalayas. It was 1,000 miles (1,600 km) long and built with hand tools. Nothing was more important to the Chinese army during the war; it was their only route for obtaining supplies.

The other goods news came from Columbia University: Wu was asked to stay on. She was carving out a career in nuclear physics that was, after the end of the war, a field in which there were virtually no industrial jobs, so a university position was her only option. In the university system, faculty members usually start out as assistant professors. They do not really "assist" anyone; they are given a contract, renewable annually, for six years. If their research is judged to be good enough, they are given tenure and promoted to associate professor. If they are not tenured, they must leave the university. Once a person receives tenure, it is very difficult for that person to be fired. This was built into the system as a protection to the faculty members so they could pursue their research and publish their results without fear of political reprisals. After a span of about 10 years, if associate professors win national or international acclaim, they can be promoted to full professor, usually with a hefty raise in salary.

Wu was not in this system. She was in the shadowy class of research professor, where different universities have different rules, tenure can be as elusive as a single nucleus, and salary, which comes from external sources, is not guaranteed. Nevertheless, she had a good lab and was in a position to pursue almost any line of research she thought to be worthwhile. But, what should she choose?

Several Smaller Problems

Many physicists continue the research they begin as a graduate student. In order to obtain a Ph.D. in physics, besides passing the courses and special tests designed to ensure the candidate's complete knowledge of the field, a requirement for the Ph.D. is that the student become an expert in the field, discovering things that have never been known before. This knowledge is promulgated through publications in technical journals, and since the successful students have devoted so much energy to a particular line of research and are already experts, they often continue in this field. Following this vein, Wu could have continued studying the decay chains of other nuclei. Had she done this, Wu might have been completely forgotten by now.

The nuclear research that began with Rutherford and then progressed to the use of the cyclotron represented the most promising line of work. It became clear that the biggest mysteries in physics lie at the nuclear level. The class of physics that describes nature at these incredibly small distances is quantum mechanics. Quantum mechanics was still a relatively new discipline at the time, and there were various theories being proposed to describe the different reactions that were observed. One of these reactions was beta decay, the emission of an electron or a positron from a nucleus, which was a very strange phenomenon. It was known that the nucleus consists solely of protons and neutrons, yet in beta decay, out comes an electron.

While at Berkeley, Wu had studied the decay chain of a number of different kinds of nuclei and was quite familiar with beta decay, one of the several ways in which a nucleus can decay. In 1933, Fermi had developed a theory of beta decay, and physicists around the world had been trying to do experiments to verify, or disprove, Fermi's theory. It was an exciting and wild time in nuclear physics; various labs were reporting different results. No one knew if Fermi's theory was correct or whether the experimentalists were disproving it. The only time physicists are sure they understand something is when the experiments agree with the theory, and this was definitely not the case.

The Nobel Prize winner and theoretical physicist Chen Ning Yang (1922–   ), who would soon carry out a very important collaboration with Wu, once said, "If you choose the right problem, you get important results that transform our perception of the underlying structure of the universe," according to Sharon McGrayne's *Nobel Prize Women in Science*. Wu struggled with this issue. Ever since her early days in China, she wanted to "transform our perception of the underlying structure of the universe." They were not her words, but they were her sentiments. She also stressed, according to *Nobel*

Prize Women in Science, that, "You must know the purpose of the research exactly, what you want to get out of it, and what point you want to show." This quote gives an interesting glimpse into her character. Not all physicists share this view. Some feel that for true, basic research the purpose may not be known, and the researcher may not know what to get out of it. But, Wu was practical; she followed these guidelines, and they turned out to be very helpful to her career.

During this period, as Wu searched for the right problem, she was still being productive. There are always a number of questions that need the attention of a good experimental physicist, and during this period in her career, she did a number of important but not groundbreaking experiments. One of the most prestigious technical journals, then and now, is *Physical Review Letters.* The title might be deceptive: The articles are not "letters" in the traditional sense but are research articles that are short and timely and important to a broad class of physicists. During this time, Wu enjoyed publishing letters, often with other authors, sometimes alone.

Race-car drivers are always looking for the ace mechanic who can make any engine run better. Wu was becoming the "ace mechanic" for experimental physicists, always improving the detectors, always making the equipment run better. In her lab at Columbia, she worked night and day on the neutron spectrometer. In chapter 1, the spectrometer, an instrument that measures the speed or energy of charged particles, was discussed. A neutron spectrometer measures the energy of neutrons. The existing neutron spectrometers were not good enough to discern the sometimes subtle energy differences between neutrons that are emitted from radioactive nuclei, so Wu decided to put an end to this unacceptable state of affairs.

In order to improve the spectrometer, Wu made the components more efficient and increased their sensitivity. She also redesigned the device so that twice as many measurements could be taken at one time and updated the electronics so it could respond in microseconds. Using this, she was able to measure and characterize neutrons emitted from radioactive forms of cadmium, iridium, and silver. These experiments were not earthshaking, but they improved the state of knowledge about nuclear physics and buttressed her growing reputation for being careful and precise.

Another problem to steal Wu's attention was the issue concerning the range of nuclear forces. The electric force between charged particles is said to be of infinite range, but it was evident that nuclear forces, the forces that hold the neutrons and protons together in the

Always at home in the lab, Wu here can be seen in her Columbia laboratory in 1963.
(University Archives, Columbia University)

nucleus, are short-range forces, a few fermi (femtometers) at most. One of the leading theoretical physicists at that time was Julian Schwinger (1918–94), who worked under Oppenheimer at Berkeley for a while but went to Harvard University after the war, where he would perform some of his most important research. Schwinger had calculated that nuclear forces should have a range of either 0 or 8 fermi, but neither seemed right. Using her newly designed spectrometer, Wu found that the range of the nuclear force was about 3 fermi, a result that was accepted by the physics community. This was another useful result she published as a letter, but she was still looking for "right problem," the problem that would propel her to the top of the field.

Wu Chooses Beta Decay

Finally, Wu decided that beta decay seemed to be the perfect problem. If she could bring her skills to bear on the worldwide problem of beta decay, perhaps she could settle the issue and decide whether Fermi's theory was correct. It was known that the emitted electrons could have any energy between 0 and 0.6 MeV. Fermi's theory predicted the precise energy spectrum of the emitted electrons. This means that if 1,000 electrons were observed, the theory predicted how many had an energy of 0.1 MeV, how many had an energy of 0.2 MeV, and so on. This energy spectrum was a firm prediction of Fermi's theory, but it was not what experimentalists measured. Many of the observed electrons had far less energy than Fermi's theory predicted, and with all of the divergent data and disagreement with theory, no one knew what to think about decay.

During World War II, beta decay did not seem as important as other problems. Refining uranium, developing radar systems, and related military issues captured the interest and funding of most research organizations. With the end of the war, research could go back to attacking the more fundamental problems. At the time, one of the most fundamental issues was beta decay. Experimental results were not uniform and did not confirm Fermi's theory. Yet, there was no other viable theory of beta decay, and Fermi's theory seemed to be a very straightforward application of quantum mechanics.

Particles, Antiparticles, and Spin

All of the materials and compounds in existence were known to be made of the 92 elements, and before 1932, all of the elements were known to consist of three particles—the electron, the proton, and the neutron. To a physicist, this is a simple and beautiful picture of the world in which the complex and varied characteristics of the myriad substances that are observed are all explained in terms of only three elementary particles. The beauty of this picture was marred in 1932 when Carl Anderson (1905–91) discovered a particle that had the mass of an electron but had a positive charge, opposite to the negatively charged electron. Anderson named this particle the *positron,* or *antiparticle,* and today it is known that nearly all particles have antiparticles. For example, the antiproton has the same mass as the proton but is negatively charged.

Besides charge, particles are endowed with another intrinsic quantity—spin. This spin, coupled with the charge, gives the particle a *magnetic moment,* a term physicists use to say that the particle creates a magnetic field that is much like the field of a simple, but extremely small bar magnet. According to the rules of quantum mechanics, once an axis is established, the spin can point either along the axis (parallel) or in the opposite direction (antiparallel), but nowhere else. Physicists usually describe this as saying that spin can be either up (parallel) or down (antiparallel). When a neutron and an antineutron are created as a pair, if the neutron has spin up, the antineutron will have spin down, and vice versa. The same is true for all particles and antiparticles with spin, such as the electron and the proton.

Although the discovery of antiparticles doubled the number of known particles, soon a host of other particles would be discovered. The muon, which is like a heavy electron, was discovered in 1937, and the long sought-after neutrino was found in 1956. In addition, a whole class of particles called "mesons" would be discovered over the years. The proliferation of new particles was so great and diverse that physicists referred to them as the elementary particle "zoo."

Of all the new particles that were discovered, the one of the most importance to Wu was the positron. When she did her experiments on beta decay, she looked at both the electrons and positrons that were emitted. This was one of the reasons her experiments were better than all others. Another important particle to Wu was one of the mesons, the K meson (kaon), which played an important role in her future.

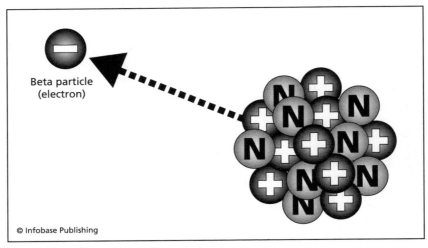

In beta decay, the nucleus emits an electron.

To Wu, it was not enough to do an experiment carefully; if other people were getting different results, she felt it was important to explain why they were getting the wrong result. She believed that the radioactive sources that others were using were too thick and that many of the electrons, after being emitted in the beta decay process, would ricochet from other atoms, losing their energy as they did. This would account for why so many experiments were getting different results. Varying thicknesses would mean the beta electrons would have unlike amounts of materials to pass through and would thereby lose different amounts of energy. But, there was a problem.

The spectrometers that were in use employed a large iron core. The iron is useful for making a large magnetic field, which is essential in the use of a spectrometer. These kinds of spectrometers required that the source of the beta electrons (that is, the radioactive material) have a small area and at the same time produce many electrons. The only way to satisfy both of the conditions was to have a thick source. This is because the radioactive materials were made as a film of copper sulfate ($CuSO_4$) that covers a slide, and in order to get many electrons, this film had to be thick. This, Wu suspected, was the problem. Thick sources were used in order to get a large enough number of electrons to measure, but they are what caused the energy losses to the electrons.

Wu's solution to this conundrum was to eschew the existing spectrometer. She had already redesigned other spectrometers and was no stranger to ingenuity and hard work. Instead of using the iron core spectrometer, Wu redesigned an older spectrometer that used a coil of wire, called a "solenoid." Leon Lidofsky, one of her first graduate students, described her ingenious solution as follows:

> As the Pupin Laboratories were being brought back to their prewar condition, Wu had discovered an iron-free solenoidal beta-spectrometer that had been placed in storage to make space for the wartime research. She recognized the potential advantages it could offer. Together with several of her graduate students, she brought the solenoidal spectrometer back to operating condition and modified its design to optimize its transmission and to permit the use of large-area, hence thinner, sources. They worked on techniques to disperse the source

Wu with the particle accelerator at Columbia in 1963 (Robert W. Kelley/Time Life Pictures/Getty Images)

material as uniformly as possible to minimize the maximum source thickness. Finally, they placed those sources onto very thin, electrically-conducting backings to avoid back-scatter and source charging.

Lidofsky refers to another key point in her work: Not only were the films to be thin; they had to have a uniform thickness. Wu, in addition to the rest of her innovations, learned how to make these very thin films with uniform thickness. How did she do this? In her own words, from *Physical Review*, 1949, "A more uniform source can be obtained by adding a trace of detergent to the $CuSO_4$ solution." Sometimes a little soap can go a long way.

Wu Continues to Receive Acclaim

The question lingered in Wu's mind, Are the sources thin enough? Wu wanted to be absolutely sure she was correct. She wanted to establish the reputation of being precise, accurate, and correct. So, she was not content simply to hope the sources were thin enough. In a brainstorm, Wu decided to use both electron and positron (antielectron) emitters and predicted the energy spectrum for each. If there were interactions due to the thickness of the source, these predictions would differ from the experimental findings, and they would be off in different ways. When Wu performed the experiment, both predictions were correct, and the infamous problem of beta decay was finally solved. After that, other laboratories around the world learned how to make thin films of the radioactive materials and verified her results.

As noted above, Wu was not satisfied to do an experiment carefully. She preferred to show why others had obtained the wrong answer. To verify that her hypothesis about the thick sources was correct, Wu actually made thick sources and measured the energy spectrum to show explicitly how the results varied. As she said in her 1949 article from *Physical Review*, "We have investigated the spectrum of the three beta emitters having radically different spectrum shapes, under exactly the same experimental conditions except for the thickness of the source." There remained some doubts, so Wu solved the problem.

This example illustrates some of the characteristics that made Wu such an exemplary experimental physicist. While other physicists simply redid the existing experiments, often replicating the setup others used, Wu went her own way. She used and designed new instruments to measure what no one else could. When she announced that the electrons were emitted with precisely the energy spectrum Fermi had predicted, she became known around the world for her expertise. The result demonstrated her prowess in picking the right problem. As Yang said, "If you choose the right problem, you get important results that transform our perception of the underlying structure of the universe," and Wu did this. In the words of Lidofsky, "I had joined her group around that time. One of my first assigned tasks was to develop techniques for preparing very uniform sources. I prepared sources for some of those studies, and helped in the measurements of the spectra as well. The degree of agreement between the measured and predicted spectra for this variety of spectra clearly established the validity of the Fermi theory."

As Nobel laureate William A. Fowler (1911–95), a physicist at California Institute of Technology, noted, according to *Nobel Prize Women in Science,* "[Wu's] beta decay work was important for its incredible precision." Tsung-Dao Lee, who won the Nobel Prize in physics for his work on parity, is quoted in *Chien-shiung Wu, Pioneering Physicist and Atomic Researcher* as saying, "C. S. Wu was one of the giants in physics. In the field of beta decay, she had no equal."

Wu's result was so important that some physicists felt she should have been nominated for the Nobel Prize. Beta decay had been observed for decades, and it was more than 10 years since Fermi had developed the theory that predicted the energy spectrum. Physicists throughout the United States and Europe had worked on the problem, which only seemed to get worse as the years went on. Wu's elegant and decisive experiment solved one of the most important enigmas in the world of physics. What, therefore, should be more appropriate than the Nobel Prize in recognition? However, the rules of the prize require it to be awarded for a discovery, and although Wu's work was outstanding, she did not discover anything new. To some, the Nobel Prize was more attributable to those who were adept in the politics of science. Robert Marc Friedman, in *The Politics of Excellence,* writes: "The mid-1940s Nobel Prizes were not awarded on the basis of recognizing merit; instead, they had become to a great extent instruments in the politics of science." Later in her career, the issue of the Nobel Prize would once again raise its political head.

5

Professor Wu

As the middle of the 20th century approached, Wu continued to work on important experiments dealing with beta decay. Her vigilant work in the laboratory helped clear up nagging problems about fundamental physics that had gone unsettled for years. Her detailed experiments also helped decide which of existing theories were correct.

Two Theories of Beta Decay

The previous chapters of this volume discussed beta decay (electron or positron emission from a nucleus) and Wu's great accomplishment of proving Fermi's theory correct. However, many years had passed between the publication of that theory and Wu's experiment. When this type of situation occurs in physics—a conflict between

Wu with two of her important tools at the Columbia lab: a pencil and the accelerator (0945.Wu, ChienShiung)

theory and experiment—theoreticians as well experimentalists go to work. Theoretical physicists ponder the most basic concepts in nature and carefully examine the fundamental tenets upon which the theory was built. Pauli, who earlier postulated the existence of the neutrino, showed that there could be only five forms of interaction that participate in the nuclear forces. These go by the following out-landish-sounding names: scalar, pseudoscalar, vector, axial vector, and tensor. These five forms are described in the sidebar, but here the essential point is that the long and tortuous years of disagree-ment between theory and experiment spurred physicists to examine the most basic ideas of beta decay. More experiments were needed to determine the true nature of the nucleus, and Wu was ready to do the work.

No one was more interested in beta decay than Wu, who had built her reputation by showing that the Fermi theory was correct. One can imagine her thoughts as she contemplated the possibility of this new interaction. She must have believed that the Fermi theory was correct, at least initially, yet now Gamow and other theoreticians were saying another interaction might be at work deep inside the inscrutable nucleus. Perhaps she began to doubt earlier results. In her previous work, she studied the beta emission from copper atoms, but she understood one nucleus can be extremely different from

Five Interactions

At first glance, one might imagine that there could be a limitless number of the kinds of nuclear forces that can exist. However, when physicists apply essential stipulations to the theory, it is found that there can be only five kinds of nuclear interactions. Physicists named these according to the technical terms that describe them (*scalar, pseudoscalar, vector, axial vector,* and *tensor*). For example, a vector quantity is one that has both magnitude and direction. An example of a vector is velocity: A driver traveling 50 miles per hour (80 kmh) due north has magnitude (50 mph) and direction (north). Temperature is an example of a scalar quantity, one that has magnitude but no direction. An axial vector is like a vector, except that if it were viewed in a mirror, it would change sign. This means, for example, if one views a slowing rotating fan in a mirror, it will appear to spin in the opposite direction. The same idea holds for the pseudoscalar. Finally, the tensor interaction is more general than the vector interaction and is sometimes thought of as a vector multiplied by a vector.

These kinds of interactions are important for a couple of reasons. First, since there are only five of them, physicists can test theories for each kind of putative interaction by trial and error. (Imagine trying to do this if there were 5 million kinds of interactions!) Second, the idea of a pseudo quantity (that is, one that changes sign under a reflection) is very important in beta decay as will be seen in chapter 6.

another. Just as different atoms or molecules can behave differently, different nuclei can be quite diverse. For example, some are stable and some decay, and different nuclei decay into different particles with different half-lives. For this reason, it was unknown whether the Gamow-Teller mechanism existed.

By now, Wu had established herself as an authority on beta decay, and nothing would be more natural than for her to delve into this topic. Not only was her reputation at stake, there was a growing interest in the topic of the two interactions, so she began to search for the right kind of experiment. Wu concluded that ^{6}He (helium-6), with two additional neutrons, held the answer. In a 1952 publication in *Physical Review,* she stated: "The beta-spectrum of He^6 is of great theoretical interest." Wu went about preparing this experiment with her trademark meticulousness and forethought. She used Columbia's magnetic solenoidal spectrometer with which she was thoroughly familiar. This was placed 50 feet (15 m) from the cyclotron in order to eliminate possible stray magnetic fields. In her description of the experiment, she explained: "The cyclotron was turned on for five seconds. A half-second later, the spectrometer and monitor GM [Geiger] counters were turned on for five seconds. . . . Under these conditions the radioactive purity of the source was greater than 98 percent."

Perhaps the most surprising part of this work was her result: It was inconclusive! Although she noted that the Fermi interaction had to exist, the amount of the Gamow-Teller was still uncertain. Wu was experiencing something typical in the life of an experimental physicist: Even a well-designed experiment may not give the definitive results that are hoped for or needed. This kind of outcome is something that Wu was not likely to forget. As she planed future experiments, she would try to ensure that the results were much more predictive, and much more powerful, than what she obtained here. In time, other researchers would find that some nuclei do indeed exhibit the Gamow-Teller transition, but Wu would soon move on to more important things.

The Family Grows

Wu and Yuan were married in 1942, and five years later, they had a son whom they named Vincent. The family resided in an apartment on Claremont Avenue, two blocks from the main campus of Columbia University. The proximity to the campus gave Wu every opportunity to get to her beloved lab, which was perhaps the main reason she would live there for more than 50 years.

In many marriages, especially at the time, a woman would give up her professional career to raise a child, but not Wu. She was completely engulfed in her research on beta rays, working day and night in the Pupin Labs at Columbia, and would not be stopped by having a son. Wu had trouble taking any time away from her work and found it difficult to abandon her research for even a single night. In a well-known story, according to McGrayne's *Nobel Prize Women in Science,* her students devised a plan to keep her out of the lab for an entire evening. They hoped to get some work done without her tinkering with the equipment. Thinking their plan was foolproof, the students bought her and Vincent tickets to a children's movie and set about working alone for the evening. They quickly realized that their plan had failed. Wu walked into the lab ready for work, explaining that she gave her ticket to her nursemaid.

Wu's former student Koller said: "It was very exciting, but she was rough—very demanding. She pushed the students until they did it right. Everything had to be explained to the last decimal. She was never satisfied. She wanted people to work late at night, early in the morning, all day Saturday, all day Sunday, to do things faster, to never take time off," according to McGrayne.

Although some of her students thought that Wu did not spend enough time with Vincent, it is always difficult to compare different

Wu's son, Vincent Yuan (AIP Emilio Segrè Visual Archives; Leo James Rainwater)

Wu may have worked in the lab night and day, but here she is smiling (AIP Emilio Segrè Visual Archives, Segrè Collection)

eras. Today it is commonplace for woman to get back to work soon after giving birth, often leaving the child in daycare or with family. What is acceptable today could be viewed with condemning eyes in the past. However, McGrayne quotes a former student as saying, "She worked late at night. Her son would call and say he was hungry. He'd call and call. Then the next day she'd say how great her son was, he was so hungry that he'd opened a can of spaghetti and eaten it." Vincent, who is now a physicist at Los Alamos National Laboratory, was not fazed. He has said: "It was an okay way to grow up."

Wu always pushed herself hard, a work habit she also expected from her students. Taking time off from the lab was anathema to her: She even frowned on a student who stayed away for a religious holiday. Her friend Ursula Lamb noted: "I think her slave-driving in part came because she was aware of what it took to succeed." Lamb continued:

> *She was a slave driver. She was abrupt and rough, and maybe more rough than an American would be. If something annoyed her, if she felt that a student was performing below*

par, she gave him hell, because she was anxious that he wasn't going to make it. But maybe her students wouldn't allow for that. They'd take the words but not the spirit. Her manner of being abrupt is being personal and caring in a way that is simply different. For her to break through her politeness and to tell somebody something honestly is a measure of compassion and caring—not aggression, as it is in the United States.

In October 1934, award-winning cartoonist Milton Caniff began a syndicated cartoon series called *Terry and the Pirates.* In the series, an American boy, Terry, goes to China and fights against villainous adversaries. One of the fiercest of these is the femme fatale, Dragon Lady. Physicists and students alike must have been aware of this character because Wu had acquired this nickname from her colleagues and students. While Dragon Lady is certainly not as endearing as Courageous Hero, Lidofsky said that outsiders used it more than her students, as stated in McGrayne's biography.

Theories Confirmed

Wu had bigger things on her mind than epithets. In fact, she began thinking about one of the most energetic processes in the universe—particle-antiparticle annihilation. For example, if 1 kilogram (2.2 pounds) of matter could be mixed with 1 kilogram of antimatter, the energy released would be more than 2,000 times the amount of energy that was released in the atomic bomb that was dropped over Hiroshima. In the previous chapter it was stated that, in general, particles have antiparticles, such as the electron and positron. These two particles have the same mass, but everything else about them is "opposite." What this essentially means is that if they come together, they can completely annihilate each other and, through Einstein's famous formula $E = mc^2$, be turned into pure energy. The term *pure energy* means that the mass is converted to photons, energetic particles much like some of the cosmic rays that continually bombard the Earth.

Like Wu's son, Vincent, this exciting area of physics was still in its infancy, and there were predictions of the theory that remained untested. An untested theory, especially one involving elementary particles, must have rung bells for Wu as loud as any Pavlov's dogs heard. Wu heard the bell proclaiming an unproven theory and started to design an experiment that could confirm, or disprove, the theory. This is another example of how progress is made in science. Sometimes a string of observations is made, and the data, analyzed and modeled, are in search of a theory. At other times, like the case

Parity

The most important concept in physics that relates to Wu's greatest success is parity. To understand Wu's greatest achievement, it is necessary to understand parity.

Consider a student who is holding a spinning top. It is not spinning too fast, so the student can easily determine which way it is rotating. Suppose it is rotating in clockwise direction. Now, suppose the student is observing the top in a mirror. Which way does the mirror image appear to rotate? She will observe it to rotate in the opposite, or in this case, counterclockwise, direction. This is an easy experiment to do, and the reader is urged to try it (any rotating object will do). The fact that the mirror image is different from the true object is not surprising to anyone who has tried to read words in a mirror. A parity transformation is how physicists describe the process of looking in a mirror.

Another way to view the difference between an object and its mirror image is by "handedness." If a person looks at his mirror image and raises his right hand, the mirror image will appear to be that same person raising the left hand. Thus, one may say that a parity transformation changes a right-handed system to a left-handed system.

The concept of parity in atomic physics was originally introduced in 1924 by Otto Laporte (1902–71), an eclectic physicist who was elected posthumously to the National Academy of Sciences. He was describing how atoms emit light, and by assigning a parity to each state of the system, he showed that parity is conserved (does not change) when an atom emits a photon. If parity is conserved, this means the process would appear to be exactly the same in the mirror. In the case of the spinning top experiment, parity is not conserved; the mirror image is different from the actual process. However, at the atomic level, things are different, and as Laporte showed, nature seems to conserve parity. In 1927, Wigner at hand, it is the other way around. The photons created in the anni-hilation of the electron and positron had certain characteristics pre-dicted from the theory, but no one had ever tested it. No one knew if the theory was right.

These characteristics were the states of polarization. Today, almost everyone has heard of polarization thanks to sunglasses and

extended this to a fundamental principle. He proved that all interac-tions involving the electromagnetic field conserve parity. At the atomic level, nature seems to conserve parity, and for the next few decades, this was taken to be an unassailable truth.

Physicists use conservation laws to help guide them to describe the fundamental forces and interactions in nature. Other conservation laws include conservation of energy and conservation of charge. In order to model nuclear interactions, physicists also used conservation of parity to describe the kinds of forces that were allowed. In 1994, 60 of the leading scientists around the world met in Erice, Sicily, at an event called The International Conference on the History of Original Ideas and Basic Discoveries in Particle Physics. Wu was invited to talk about parity, and this is how she described it, according to *History of Original Ideas and Basic Discoveries in Particle Physics*:

> The law of parity invariance states: no new physical law should result from the construction of a new system differing from the original by being a mirror image. That is, there is no absolute distinction between a real object and its mirror image. In other words, two worlds, one based upon a right handed system (say, real object) and one based upon a left-handed system (say, mirror image) obey the same laws of physics. This law had been built into all physical theories from the 1920's to 1957 and has severely restricted the predicted behavior of elementary particles.

Just as Laporte had done earlier, physicists began to assign parity to all of the elementary particles they discovered. The rule of conservation of parity was held to be valid for about 30 years, until, in one of the most famous and important experiments of all time, Wu showed that parity is not conserved. This will be the subject of chapter 6.

antiglare lenses. The direction of polarization is actually the direction of the electric field, which is the essence of the light. In the photons created in the annihilation, the theory predicted that the polarizations of the created photons were at right angles to each other and that the ratio of one polarization to the other was precisely a factor of two. If Wu could devise the right experiment, she would prove a fundamental and important theory about particle-antiparticle interactions.

Others had tried the experiment. One group had obtained error bars (uncertainties) so large that the results were nearly useless, and another group had found a result that was smaller than the theory predicted. The warring parties of theory and experiment found no truce, but Wu was confident she could settle the issue.

To perform the experiment, Wu fired up the cyclotron at Columbia University. She used a radioactive form of copper to obtain the positrons, smashed them into electrons, and placed counters and detectors carefully around the apparatus to measure the photons. In the course of 30 continuous hours of operation, she kept one detector fixed while moving the other in a great arc, and then repeated this after interchanging the detectors. The result of her experiment was that the ratio of the two polarizations was 2.04, very close to the theoretical value of 2.0. In her words, in a publication of *Physical Review* in 1950, "Therefore, the agreement is very satisfactory."

Typically, although the university pays the salary of professors, it does not generally provide funds for the purchase of equipment (other than start-up funds). The physicist must therefore find external financial support, and in research universities, physicists will usually be denied tenure if they do not secure such funding. In 1946, the Atomic Energy Commission was created after the congressional declaration that atomic energy should not be limited to defense. (The Atomic Energy Commission was abolished in 1974 when President Gerald Ford signed the Energy Reorganization Act.) Wu quickly secured funding from the commission for her research on a radioactive form of lead, what used to be called radium D (RaD). Until 1939, it was assumed that the decay of this element was understood, but as better measurements were made, this simple substance opened a storm of controversy. Physicists used different instruments and tried different modes of decay, but no two experiments agreed. In Wu's own words from her article in *Physical Review* in 1953, "After another decade with cloud chambers, curved crystal spectrometers, proportional counters, and sodium iodide scintillation counters seven gamma rays were observed in RaD, and several modes of its complex decay were proposed, but none of them were certain." With her usual care and expertise, Wu was able to measure the gamma rays and the electrons that were emitted and settled the complicated controversy that surrounded the decay of RaD.

However, there was something much more important going on than the issue of RaD decay. At the time, Maria Goeppert-Mayer (1906–72) was working on her theory of the shell model of the nucleus. This work developing the theory that describes the energy levels of nuclei would earn her the Nobel Prize in 1963. In this description, the nuclei were assigned values of intrinsic parity, just as Otto Laporte had done for atoms (see sidebar). In Wu's work on RaD, she had to consider the parity of the nucleus, an extremely important step for her. Her familiarity with parity would be essential, and in the following chapter, it will be seen how forthcoming experiments of Wu's would alter how the scientific world viewed parity.

A Chance to Go Home

During this period, Wu had an opportunity to return to her beloved China. The National Central University of China had offered not only her a position but also to her husband, Yuan. Such double offers were very rare and are still difficult to arrange to this day, so the chance to work near her husband and the family she had left behind would seem to be an attractive opportunity. But, Wu refused. The officials at the National Central University gave Wu another year to stay in the United States, hoping that she and Yuan could gather up equipment to take to China, but she still refused.

Chiang Kai-shek in Taiwan and the Communist Party in mainland China were solidifying their control. At the same time, the United States was denying reentry visas to anyone who went to a Communist country. Thus, if Wu went back to China, she might not have been allowed back in the United States. Wu was still able to keep in touch with her father, and she turned to him for advice. As much as he wanted to see her, he believed it was not a good time for her to return and advised her to stay in the United States. Wu took her father's advice long ago when he told her to "Put your head down and just keep walking forward," and she took his advice this time also. She and her husband stayed in the United States and became U.S. citizens in 1954.

Staying in the United States was not a bad decision. Wu had a good position at Columbia and was able to work on her research night and day. In fact, when she was hired as a research faculty member at this prestigious university, Wu was ecstatic. She had fared better than other female physicists of the time. For example, even Goeppert-Mayer, who was six years older than Wu, did not have such a position. The advantage of being a research scientist was that Wu could spend all of her time on research. But, without teaching duties, she was considered to be somewhat outside the mainstream of the faculty and did not receive the kinds of promotion discussed earlier in this volume. This changed in 1952 when Wu became associate professor at Columbia University. To help her get promoted, William Havens, director of the Nuclear Physics Laboratory at Columbia, came to her aid. Havens was convinced that Wu had extraordinary abilities and said later, "She was the world's most distinguished woman physicist of her time." Havens arranged for her to teach some courses. This, he knew, would get her more recognition both among the students and faculty. With this and her greatest achievement yet to come, Wu would be made full professor in 1958.

6

Parity, the Experiment That Changed Physics

The infamous theta-tau problem perplexed the entire physics community. The theta particle and the tau particle had been discovered in 1949, and while some kinds of measurements seemed to indicate that they were really one and the same particle, others showed that they must be two different particles. If they were really the same particle, then the long-held belief that parity is conserved had to be abandoned. This idea was so outrageous that some physicists openly bet it was wrong. Wu went about performing her most famous experiment that proved parity was not conserved, causing some colleagues to lose their bets and eat their hats and forever changing how we see the world.

Wu and her "mirror" image (AIP Emilio Segrè Visual Archives)

The Theta-Tau Puzzle

With the end of World War II, physicists became less interested in the wartime research of making atomic bombs. Even though the terrible burden of creating the atomic bomb was lifted, the legacy of nuclear physics left its imprint. As bigger and more powerful cyclotrons were built, experimenters found they had enough energy to create new particles—particles never before seen—and the simple world of protons, neutrons, and electrons became an illusion of the past. Many of these particles had a mass somewhere in the range between that of a proton and electron, but little else was known about these strange newcomers. So little was known about them that their names would change as fast as new particles were discovered.

Today, the lay and professional environments understand the structure of particles much better. For example, most of the particles one observes are made of four basic particles—the electron and three quarks, called by the somewhat whimsical names of the up quark (u), the down quark (d), and the strange quark (s). In general, q stands for "quark," and $\bar{q}$ stands for "antiquark." The following table shows how some of the particles we observe are formed from these building blocks.

Particle	Constituents
Proton	u u d
Neutron	u d d
Pi meson (pion)	q q̲
K meson	d s̲

Note: The stable particles are the u, d, and s quarks and the electron. The other particles live only a very short time and then decay into the stable particle and photons. The Pi meson (pion) and K meson were some of the newcomers to the world of elementary particles.

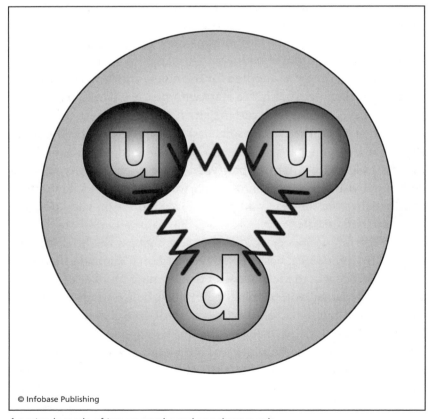

A proton is made of two up quarks and one down quark.

In the early 1950s a number of particles called "mesons" were discovered. Although they were mysterious then, now they are understood to be a pair consisting of a quark and an antiquark. Two examples of mesons are given in the table above. Another kind of particle that was discovered at this time was the muon. It is nothing like a meson and is not made up of quarks; instead, it may be viewed as a heavy electron. These differences were not understood in the 1950s, which created the confusion involving their nomenclature. To add to the confusion, the Pi meson came to be called the "pion," even though it is nothing at all like the muon.

During this period two similar particles were found: the theta meson and the tau meson. The theta meson decayed into two pions, while the tau meson decayed into three pions. As more measurements were made, it was observed that the theta meson and the tau meson had the same mass and the same lifetime. Generally, that would be a signal that the two mesons were really the same particle. However, just as Laporte had assigned parity to different particles, the same procedure was adopted for the pions, and it was known that the theta meson decayed into a state with positive parity, but the tau meson decayed into a state with negative parity. This was the puzzle: On the one hand, the two mesons had the same mass and therefore should be the same particle, but on the other hand, they could decay into particles with different parity. In other words, parity was not conserved. But, conservation of parity was a rock solid rule in physics, unchallenged for nearly 40 years. This conundrum was known as the "tau-theta puzzle."

On April 3, 1956, nearly 200 physicists met for the Sixth Annual Rochester Conference, held in New York. One of the main themes of the conference was to make sense of the puzzling number of particles that were observed and to solve the mystery concerning the issue of the theta and tau particles. If parity was not conserved, they should be one and the same particle and the mystery apparently solved, but like a skunk at a picnic, this idea was hard to accept. One of the greatest theoretical physicists of the 20th century was Nobel Prize winner Richard Feynman (1918–88) (see sidebar). He attended this meeting and questioned the notion of parity conservation, planting a seed of doubt that grew quickly. The following is a fascinating account of the very genesis of this idea from Andrzej K. Wróblewski in his book *The Downfall of Parity—The Revolution That Happened Fifty Years Ago*:

> *Richard Feynman, who was a participant, gave a lively recollection of the event: "I was sharing a room with a guy named Martin Block, an experimenter. And one evening he said to me, 'Why are you guys so insistent on this parity rule? Maybe the tau and theta are the same particle. What would be the consequences if the parity rule were wrong?'*
>
> *I thought a minute and said, 'It would mean that nature's laws are different for the right hand and the left hand, that there's a way to define the right hand by physical phenomena. I don't know that that's so terrible, though there must be some bad consequences of that, but I don't know. Why don't you ask the experts tomorrow?'*
>
> *He said, 'No, they won't listen to me. You ask.'*
>
> *So the next day at the meeting . . . I got up and said, 'I'm asking this question for Martin Block: What would be the consequences if the parity rule was wrong?'*
>
> *[Tsung-Dao] Lee, of Lee and [Chen Ning] Yang, answered something complicated, and as usual I didn't understand very well. At the end of the meeting Block asked me what he said, and I said I did not know, but as far as I could tell, it was still open—there was still a possibility. I didn't think it was likely, but I thought it was possible. . . ."*

The Sixth Annual Rochester Conference ended with no solution of the tau-theta puzzle.

By this time, physicists knew there were four kinds of fundamental forces. Since they influence aspects of everyday life, the gravitational force and the electromagnetic force are the two most well known. However, acting on a much smaller scale are two other forces, the nuclear forces, known as the "strong force" and the "weak force." The strong force is what overcomes the repulsion of all of the positive charges in the nucleus and holds it together. The weak force is responsible for beta decay. In the previous chapter, it was noted that Wigner proved that parity is conserved in electromagnetic interactions, but it was only extrapolation, and perhaps imagination, that bootstrapped this limited proof into a universal law. No such proof was ever given, for example, concerning the weak interaction. Wróblewski goes on to describe how Lee and Yang closed in on this issue as follows:

> *A few weeks after the Sixth Rochester Conference, late April or early May (1956) Lee and Yang met in New York at the White Rose Cafe near 125th and Broadway and discussed the possibility that parity could be violated in weak processes. Afterwards Lee asked his colleague from Columbia, Chien-shiung Wu, an expert in beta decay, whether she knew of any experiments related to this question. Lee and Yang soon discovered that nobody has ever proved that parity conservation was valid for weak interactions. They decided to analyze the problem thoroughly. On June 22, 1956, their paper entitled "Is Parity Conserved in Weak Interactions?" was submitted to the* Physical Review. *The editor of that journal, Samuel Goudsmit, protested against using the question mark in the title. The paper was finally published as "Question of Parity Conservation in Weak Interactions."*

Lee and Yang had circulated a preprint of this paper, and most physicists could not accept their radical ideas. Conservation of parity had been an accepted doctrine of physics for four decades, and few physicists were able to abandon such a well-known principle, especially since there was no known violation—until, perhaps, now. Wu remembers this period of time in the book *History of Original Ideas and Basic Discoveries in Particle Physics,* in which she states the following:

> *During the years 1945–52, I was completely submerged in the experimental studies of beta-decay. From 1952 on, my interest gradually turned away from beta decays to exotic atoms and bio-physics. But beta-decay was still like a dear old friend. There would always be a place in my heart reserved especially for it.*
>
> *One day in the early spring of 1956, my colleague Prof. T. D. Lee came up to my office on the 13th floor of Pupin Physics Lab. He asked me a series of questions concerning the status of the experimental knowledge of beta-decay.*

Richard Feynman, an American Theoretical Physicist

Born in Far Rockaway in Queens, New York, on May 11, 1918, Richard Feynman became a brilliant and colorful physicist, well known for his extraordinary ability to explain complicated problems. Like Albert Einstein, Feynman was, as a child, a late talker, not speaking until he was three years old, and also like Einstein, he would go on to be one of the most brilliant physicists of his time. He received a bachelor's degree from Massachusetts Institute of Technology in 1939. After receiving a perfect score on the entrance exam, Feynman went to Princeton University, where he received a Ph.D. in physics in 1942.

Feynman was invited to work on the Manhattan Project in Los Alamos (discussed in chapter 3), where he demonstrated both his mathematical skills and extraordinary abilities in physics. For example, even though he was considered a junior physicist, he developed, with Nobel laureate Hans Bethe (1905–2005), the Bethe-Feynman formula that predicted the yield of an atomic bomb. Feynman was promoted to be a group leader by Bethe.

During his lifetime, Feynman came to be known as an eccentric for some of his activities. At Los Alamos, Feynman would sometimes go to a lonely mesa to play his drums and chant in the style of Native Americans. He also liked to play practical jokes. He guessed that other physicists would use well-known mathematical numbers as codes to their combination locks. After trying a few different locks, Feynman was able to open some and plant mysterious letters, leading some to think there was a spy in their midst.

After the Manhattan Project ended, its director, Robert Oppenheimer, invited Feynman to go to work at Berkeley, but instead, he went with Bethe to Cornell, in Ithaca, New York. Feynman continued to show his brilliance and soon received invitations to some very prestigious universities. One of these was Princeton, which would have allowed Feynman to be at the same institution as Einstein, but Feynman chose to go to the California Institute of Technology (Cal Tech) in Pasadena. At Cal Tech, Feynman did some of his most important work. It was during this time that he helped develop quantum electrodynamics, the fundamental theory that describes how particles interact with light. He also developed a theory to help understand superfluidity, the strange state of matter when it is subject to very low temperatures. During this period, Feynman

(continues on next page)

(continued from previous page)

also did basic work on the weak interaction and, in particular, on the vector and axial couplings that were discussed in chapter 4.

One of his longest-lasting contributions to physics is known as the "Feynman diagrams," succinct sketches that show how particles interact and describe which particles are created and which are annihilated. They are so useful that they have extended beyond quantum electrodynamics and are used to help understand more modern and unproven theories, such as the speculative string theory that replaces what are believed as point particles with tiny strings.

Known as "the Great Explainer," Feynman was recognized for his teaching abilities and insistence on good and clear explanations to all students. Asked by Cal Tech to improve undergraduate teaching, Feynman began a three-year task in the early 1960s of creating lectures, culminating in the best-selling *Feynman Lectures on Physics,* which sold more than 1.5 million copies. Later, Feynman won the Oersted Medal, a prize that recognizes teaching contributions in physics.

Feynman received national recognition for his investigation of the *Challenger* disaster. On January 29, 1986, the space shuttle *Challenger* exploded 73 seconds after takeoff, killing all seven of the crew. This tragic event included a civilian, Christa McAuliffe, a teacher from Concord, New Hampshire, selected from 11,000 applicants for the first space flight ever to have a civilian aboard. Amid the grief of the nation, President Ronald Reagan appointed the Rogers Commission to investigate the catastrophe.

Wu then asked Lee if anyone had any ideas about experiments that would test the law of parity conservation. Lee said that some people had suggested using nuclei produced in nuclear reactions or from a reactor, but Wu said, "Somehow I had great misgivings about using either of these two approaches. I suggested that the best bet would be to use a ^{60}Co beta source."

This was the origin of the most important experiment of Wu's career. In order to understand Wu's ideas, the reader should remember, as explained in chapter 4, that the protons in the nucleus, all have a spin and therefore also have magnetic moments, which means that they can act like an array of miniscule magnets. Thus, if they are

Feynman, who was on the commission, took immediate objection to the way management at the National Aeronautics and Space Administration (NASA) assigned a probability of failure of the mission as one in 100,000. He pointed out that such a probability implies that NASA could launch the shuttle every day for 274 years without mishap, a number no NASA engineer took seriously. Eventually, Feynman honed in on the O-rings, the rubber seals that prevent superheated gases from escaping and harming other parts of the spacecraft. Feynman knew that it was below 30° Fahrenheit (-1° Celsius) on the day of the launch, much colder than it had been on any other launch day. A day before he was to interview a NASA manager, Feynman bought a little clamp from a local hardware store. As he questioned the manager in front of TV cameras, Feynman squeezed an O-ring that he had obtained and dropped it in a glass of ice water, which is 32°F (0°C). The manager insisted that the O-rings would maintain their resilience at the temperatures the day of the launch. If they were not resilient, they could be deformed and allow the superheated gases to escape. As the manager finished his testimony, Feynman pulled the O-rings out of the ice water and removed the clamp. The O-ring was still flattened, showing that it was not at all resilient at the temperatures the day of the launch.

Great physicists are often remembered for their contributions to their profession. This was the case for Feynman, but he was also remembered for his important analysis and explanation of the *Challenger* disaster. The shuttle program resumed 32 months after the disaster, and there have been no further troubles with O-rings.

placed in a magnetic field, the nuclei can all line up, just as a cluster of magnets would do. This will establish a net spin of the nucleus, which is assumed to be clockwise, as well as a direction of the alignment. This direction will be called up. If the spin is considered as a rotation, we know that from the discussion on parity in the last chapter, in a mirror it will appear to rotate in the opposite direction. Thus, the mirror image of this process is different than the original. If parity is conserved, then the emitted particles must emerge equally in both the up direction and the down direction. If not, then in the mirror, where the spin is reversed, things will be different. If it is different, than parity is not conserved.

The accompanying figure shows a sketch of what it would be like if parity were conserved. A sphere of cobalt nuclei is shown on the left (this world) emitting more electrons down than up. The mirror

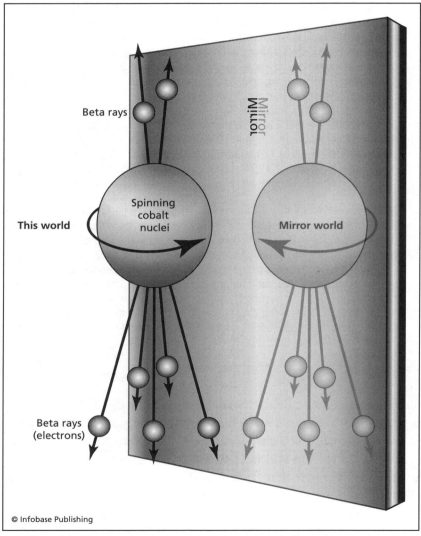

© Infobase Publishing

If parity were conserved, then the mirror image would be the same as the real image, as shown in this figure. But, this is not the case. When Wu proved that parity is not conserved, she proved that the mirror image of a fundamental process is different from the real image.

image is the same as the real image, and one cannot tell the difference between the two. This is how physicists used to think nature behaved. If parity is not conserved, then the mirror image would be reversed: More electrons would be emitted out from the top than the bottom.

In the case of the beta rays emitted by cobalt, Wu did not actually have to look in a mirror. If parity is conserved, then equal number of electrons must be emitted in the upward direction as down, thereby ensuring the mirror image is the same. If more electrons are emitted in one direction, than that signals the violation of parity.

These ideas must have been buzzing through Wu's mind on the fateful spring day in 1956 when Wu and Lee discussed the subject of parity and, in particular, parity in the realm of the weak force—beta decay. She quickly discarded the putative ideas Lee mentioned and began thinking about how to perform this parity experiment using this radioactive form of cobalt.

Anniversary Cruise

The year 1956 was the 20th anniversary of Wu's and her husband Yuan's emigration from China, and they planned a sentimental cruise to their homeland to celebrate it. They booked a cabin on the *Queen Elizabeth* and made preparations for the voyage and a well-deserved rest. It would have been the first time they shared a long restful vacation in a long while, but Yuan sailed alone. Wu knew Lee and Yang were about to submit their paper to *Physical Review.* The paper would not only state that no tests of parity conservation with the weak force had been done; the authors would also suggest a few possible tests, including the one with ^{60}Co.

It must have been a tumultuous time for Wu. Just as all the technical ideas about an experimental test of parity were pulling her to the lab, the excitement of a sentimental cruise with her husband and the expectation of seeing her family after so many years away must have been wrenching her in the opposite direction. The emotional tug-of-war did not last long, however; Wu decided to perform the experiment as soon as possible.

Her abrupt cancellation of a long-planned cruise on a special anniversary might seem surprising to some, but it is exactly what her

Near Absolute Zero

While most of the world uses the Celsius scale, in which water freezes at 0 degrees and boils at 100, the United States uses Fahrenheit. Physicists, however, use neither. They adopted the Kelvin scale, which is also called the "absolute scale." The Kelvin scale is like the Celsius, using the same increments but 273 degrees lower: For example, 0°C is -273 on the Kelvin scale.

One of the most fascinating concepts about temperature is that of absolute zero. Temperature is really a measure of the average speed of a collection of molecules or atoms. A cup of hot water, for example, is identical to a cup of cold water, except that the molecules are moving faster in the hot water. The hot cup is said to have more "thermal energy," the energy associated with the movement of the molecules. The slower the movement of the molecules, the colder the temperature. This notion suggests the idea of absolute zero, a state in which all of the molecules are absolutely still. This is 0 degrees on the Kelvin scale (0K), which is about -460°F (-273°C).

It turns out that absolute zero can never be reached, but we can get very, very close. Nitrogen, the most abundant gas in the atmosphere, turns into a liquid at 77K. Many physics and chemistry labs have supplies of liquid nitrogen to cool down specimens. Sometimes, this is just the first step in cooling. Helium gas is a liquid at 4.2K, which can be used to cool down specimens even further. Over the past decade, researchers have been able to reach a millionth of a degree kelvin, and even colder.

A sample may be cooled to less than 1K by boiling off liquid helium. This is evaporative cooling, which also occurs in the familiar situation of having water or alcohol rubbed on the skin. To reach colder temperatures, physicists had to get ingenious. The method that is used is called "adiabatic demagnetization." The idea is to turn thermal energy into magnetic energy, which is accomplished as follows. The sample is put in a strong magnetic field, hundreds of times stronger than the Earth's field, and cooled as much as possible. At this point, the sample is isolated, so no heat can flow. This is what the term *adiabatic* means—no heat flow. Next, the external magnetic field is turned off. With no magnetic field to keep them in line, the nuclei reorient themselves, but this takes energy, essentially absorbing the thermal energy used to reposition themselves. This process can be repeated again and

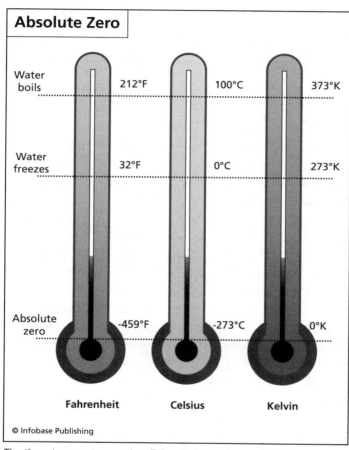

Absolute Zero

	Fahrenheit	Celsius	Kelvin
Water boils	212°F	100°C	373°K
Water freezes	32°F	0°C	273°K
Absolute zero	-459°F	-273°C	0°K

© Infobase Publishing

The three temperature scales: Fahrenheit, Celsius, and Kelvin

again, reaching temperatures into the millikelvin (one-thousandth of 1 degree) regime that Wu would need for her experiment.

In recent years, physicists have learned how to use laser beams to slow atoms even further. The coldest temperature reached using laser cooling has been in the nanokelvin (one-billionth of 1K) regime.

day-and-night work ethic called for. Wu would work late into the night, even when her son was home and hungry. On her return from a trip one night, she had the taxi drive by her lab. When she saw it was dark, she got frustrated and angry. To Wu, it was unthinkable to let equipment stand silent, unused. With this attitude toward her work and perhaps one of the biggest experiments in physics on the horizon, within her grasp, it should be no surprise that she chose to work in the lab.

The Famous Experiment

Wu knew she would need low temperatures, so she immediately set out to determine just how cold things must be for her experiment to work. The problem was that the thermal energy of the cobalt atoms was too high. If the spins could be aligned, then the thermal energy, the energy due to the random motions of the particles, would break it apart. This is like trying to keep marbles still on a wildly vibrating platform. Wu knew that if she were to align all of the cobalt atoms, she would have to cool them down so the thermal energy would not destroy the alignment. This is like keeping the hypothetical marble platform almost absolutely still. She figured that the nuclei would become aligned at about 0.01K (one one-hundredth of 1 degree kelvin). In the actual experiments, they would cool the specimen to 3 millikelvin.

In 1956, there were only two or three labs in the United States that were equipped to perform these experiments at this incredibly low temperature, and the Pupin Laboratory at Columbia could get nowhere near this chilly mark. Dr. Ernest Ambler (1923–   ), a pioneer in nuclear orientation, had recently moved from Oxford to the Low Temperature Laboratories at the National Bureau of Standards (NBS) in Washington, D.C. (after 1988, NBS became the National Institute of Standards and Technology, or NIST). The following account of Wu's first discussions with Ambler is taken from her *History of Original Ideas and Basic Discoveries in Particle Physics*: "It was on June 4, 1956 that I called and put the proposition directly to him. He accepted immediately and with enthusiasm." Instead of taking a cruise to China, Wu would be cruising between New York and Washington to set up and perform this experiment.

Wu began her work at Columbia. She prepared specimens by creating thin layers of ^{60}Co on cerium magnesium nitrate (CMN) crystals. This crystal was coated with a thin layer of cerium magnesium nitrate doped with ^{60}Co. This gave Wu the source of the beta decay, the thin layer with the radioactive cobalt. Still teaching at Columbia, too, Wu kept a very busy schedule as she shuttled back and forth.

Wu had always been careful about keeping her research secret until she was ready to publish. When visitors came to her lab, she would sometimes revert to a very poor form of English, politely respond to their questions, but say nothing of substance. Now, she was working with many more colleagues than before and did not know them as well. Yet, they had to work together in order to achieve a result the world of physics was beginning to talk about. An idea of the feelings at the time, as well of some humor, is exposed in some of the comments of the great nuclear physicist Victor Weisskopf (1908–2002) and of Lee, which appeared in Wu's *History of Original Ideas and Basic Discoveries in Particle Physics.* According to Weisskopf, "At that time Pauli was already in Europe and asked me to tell him what was happening in America, I told him that Mrs. Wu is trying to measure whether parity is conserved. He answered me, 'Mrs. Wu is wasting her time. I would bet you a large sum of money that parity is conserved.'" Pauli also wrote Weisskopf in a letter: "I do not believe that the Lord is a weak left-hander, and I am ready to bet a very large sum that the experiments will give symmetric results." By the time the letter reached Weisskopf, he already knew that parity was violated: "I could have sent Pauli a telegram that the bet was accepted. But I wrote him a letter. He said, 'I could never let it out that this is possible. I am glad that we actually did not do the bet because I can risk to lose my reputation, but I cannot risk losing my capital.'" According to Lee, "F. Bloch also declared he would eat his hat if parity were violated. And afterwards, unfortunately, he did not have a hat."

Wu was taking on an experiment that her colleagues expected to fail. The idea was too radical for many physicists. Take, for example, the great Russian physicist Lev Landau (1908–68). He had made important contributions to many areas of theoretical physics as well as to quantum mechanics, the physics that prevails at atomic and subatomic distances. He also wrote or cowrote an amazing 10 advanced textbooks in physics on a range of subjects from electromagnetism to fluid mechanics. Most of these books are still used today. Furthermore, he won the Nobel Prize in physics in 1962 for his theory that describes liquid helium, the state of helium when it is below 4.2K. Yet, in October 1956, he "maintained that parity nonconservation was an absolute nonsense," according to Wróblewski.

Wu during her famous experiment of 1957 (AIP Emilio Segrè Visual Archives, Physics Today Collection)

In fact, even Lee had doubts and had another theory ready to explain the tau-theta puzzle. In this, he supposed that the tau meson decayed into the theta meson in a very short period time so that they were really different particles. This idea did not attract much attention, but Lee was covering all bases. After Wu's experiment was completed, Lee would bury this idea as deep as other misguided attempts to explain the tau-theta puzzle.

As Wu and her colleagues made the final preparations for the experiment in Washington, it was still not clear how it would turn out. Either way, however, the result would have been useful, for it was becoming increasingly important to know whether parity was conserved in weak interactions and beta decay. The experiment was risky because there were many questions that could not be answered, and it was not known if the experiment could even be performed. If it were an easy experiment, someone would have tried it before, but it was not easy.

One problem was obtaining a way to cool the radioactive source to such low temperatures. It was not known if such an arrangement could keep the cobalt cold enough. The beta particles are absorbed very quickly in matter, so Wu had to figure out how to get the emitted particles free and not be reabsorbed by the very source they came from. Wu thought of using a thin surface layer on a crystal, which had to be on the surface of the cooling medium, the CMN crystal. She calculated that a layer 0.002 inch (0.005 mm) would do the trick, allowing most of the particles to escape. In addition, there were many other questions: how to count the electrons, where to place the detectors, what would be the effect of the external magnetic field needed to align the atoms, would this field heat up the CMN crystal? Wu's first attempt failed.

Wu needed the nuclei in the layer of ^{60}Co to stay aligned long enough so that there would be enough electrons emitted to measure in her detectors. But, within seconds, the alignment was destroyed, and the experiment could not be done. Wu suspected that the layer was warming up, perhaps from the heat of radiation or from the helium being exchanged that was used to cool the sample. She believed that the thin layer must be shielded by a thick CMN housing. She wondered "where could one obtain many large single CMN crystals in a hurry?" This indicates that Wu was feeling the pressure to finish the experiment quickly: "Relying purely on ingenuity, determination and luck, three of us (an enthusiastic chemist, a dedicated student and myself) worked together uninterruptedly to grow about ten large perfect translucent CMN single crystals by the end of three weeks. The day I carried these precious translucent crystals with me back to Washington, D.C., I was the happiest and proudest person in the whole wide world." Wu was obviously caught up in the excitement of the moment.

Finally, they were ready. Two days after Christmas in 1956, Wu was joined by the NBS staff members Ernest Ambler, Raymond W. Hayward, Dale D. Hoppes, and Ralph P. Hudson. As the detectors counted electrons and other detectors counted gamma rays, Ambler jotted down numbers is his notebook. The concrete floors and harsh lighting of the lab were accompanied by the rata-tat-tat of vacuum pumps straining to keep air away from the precious CMN crystals. The hiss of compressors from great refrigerators joined the din, making incredibly low temperatures, colder than any that exist anywhere else in the universe. But, the scientists were

Wu with other physicists at the first Mössbauer Conference (University of Illinois at Urbana-Champaign, Department of Physics, AIP Emilio Segrè Visual Archives)

quiet, wondering if they would prove what everybody expected or hit upon a real breakthrough, something that would represent a true upheaval in physics.

On December 27, an explosion of excitement was tempered by a wave of doubt. Initial results indicated the asymmetry they were searching for was real—parity was violated—but repeated experiments did not duplicate their first result. After days of careful testing and checking, Wu and her team were convinced that a smaller number of electrons were emitted in the direction of spin than in the opposite direction, the sign that parity was not conserved. Wu described the event as follows:

> *After we had finished all the experimental checks which we had set out to do we finally gathered together at two o'clock in the morning of January 9, 1957 to celebrate the great event. Dr. Hudson (head of the Low-Temp group) smilingly opened his drawer and pulled out a bottle of wine that turned out to be a Chateau Lafite-Rothschild, vintage 1949. He put it on the table with a few small paper cups. We finally drank to the overthrow of the law of parity in beta decay. On the afternoon of January 15th, the department of Physics at Columbia University called a press conference.*

That same day, they submitted two papers to *Physical Review*, and according to Wu, "The next day, the *New York Times* carried a front page headline 'Basic Concepts in Physics Reported Upset in Tests.'" As the news burst into public view and quickly spread around the world, O. R. Frisch, a professor at Cambridge University, described it in a talk at that time: "The obscure phrase 'parity is not conserved' circled the globe like a new gospel."

The impossible was possible: Parity was not conserved. This result, of course, eradicated the theta-tau issue: It was really only one particle all along, now called the "K meson." The K meson can decay two different ways because parity does not have to be conserved. Lee's backup theory was quickly forgotten, and physicists began to look at the world in a new way.

Wu's rush to solve the theta-tau puzzle was well founded. On January 4, at a meal with Columbia physicists, Leon Lederman heard about the result of December 27, the initial experiment of Wu's group that showed parity was not conserved. Lederman knew that certain decay chains of pions and muons could provide another proof of parity violation. Lederman explained his ideas over the telephone to his colleague Richard Garwin who, along with Lederman's graduate student Marcel Weinrich, fired up the university cyclotron. Swinging their massive magnets into place to control the particles, they observed particle decays that could only be explained if parity is not conserved. At 6:00 A.M. on January 8, Lederman called Lee and said, "Parity is dead."

A fascinating footnote to this historical episode is related by Wróblewski. Neither Wu nor Lederman was the first physicist to perform an experiment that tested parity conservation. The first group to follow up on the ideas of parity violation of that famous April conference in Rochester was a group in Rome, Italy: C. Castagnoli, C. Franzinetti, and A. Manfredini. They performed the same kind of experiment that Lederman did, and in describing their result, they said: "This result does not exclude an asymmetric distribution but does not suggest a strong asymmetry." They were saying that parity may not be violated, although it could be. This result was completely forgotten, and a few months later, in March 1957, they published their final results that confirmed Lederman's.

Wu's result did more than show parity is not conserved, however. It showed that basic tenets of physics, taken as gospel for decades, could be wrong. It showed that physicists cannot impose their will and prejudices on nature. It showed nothing could be taken for granted, and every precept of theoretical physics lies on a shaky support of hope and belief. If the fundamental concept of conservation of parity is wrong, what other fundamental laws of physics are incorrect?

7

Wu's Other Contributions to Particle Physics

Just after she completed the most important experiment of her career—the experiment on parity that had profound effects on how physicists view the world—Wu began to expand her expertise to other areas of experimental physics. She began to study X-rays that are emitted from atoms that, in addition to electrons, contain muons. She also undertook an experiment to test what was, at the time, one of the most controversial topics in physics—conserved current theories. Developed in part by Feynman, these theories described the weak nuclear force, the force responsible for beta decay. Wu was an expert of world renown in beta decay, and she developed another important experiment proving that this theory was correct.

Exotic Matter

The famous experiment on parity violation, described in chapter 6, was recognized worldwide as a monumental step in physics. The Nobel Prize Committee, which often takes years or decades to recognize an achievement, was quick to move, bestowing the award in 1957, but Wu was not the recipient! The Nobel Prize is awarded for making a discovery of some kind, and Wu most certainly made one as she and her coworkers discovered that parity was not conserved. Over the years, Nobel committees struggled with issues that went far beyond physics, from politics to prejudices. At the time, there was still a great deal of resentment against women physicists and women in the workforce in general. Certainly, Lee and Yang deserved credit for their careful review of the known physics, realizing that there was no evidence that parity was conserved. Sharing

Ludwig Faddeev (left), Wu, and Homer Hagstrum (right) hold awards at the American Physical Society's banquet for a 1985 Washington, D.C., meeting. (Camera Reflections by Chase Studios, courtesy AIP Emilio Segrè Visual Archives)

a Nobel Prize is common, and it might have gone to all three, Lee, Yang, and Wu. After all, she designed the experiment and made it happen, but in 1957, only two shared the prize, Lee and Yang.

An article appearing in the 2007 issue of the *Cern Courier,* an international journal of high-energy physics, quotes Yang discussing his paper of October 1956 that shows no experiments were known that violated parity. "The paper was published on 1 October 1956, and on 27 December C. S. Wu and her colleagues had the results that demonstrated that parity is violated in weak decays. Yang says that Wu contributed more than just her technical expertise: 'She did not believe the experiment would be so exciting, but believed that if an important principle had not been tested, it should be. No one else wanted to do it!'"

Wu did not complain about the prize oversight and was quick to move on to other areas of physics. Some, however, felt that she should have been included in the honor. Attributed to the 2004 edition of *American Women Scientists,* the following quote from one of her students, John McClaughry, captures the mood, as well as providing a glimpse into her classroom:

> *John McClaughry was a student in 1960 in her Advanced Nuclear Physics. He was impressed with her power of concentration under less than favorable circumstances: ". . . there was heavy construction going on outside, with lots of cement trucks backing and pouring. Prof. Wu was a tiny birdlike woman. She typically roamed back and forth, only the top third of her visible, behind the lab desk. Her English was still heavily accented, and her voice was soft. This made comprehension difficult. On a day I remember vividly, the cement trucks were in full voice outside the classroom. Prof. Wu announced that she would present the equation for some nuclear event or other. Then she turned to the blackboard, facing away from the class, and began to put terms on the board. As she added terms—eventually seven or eight, which covered at least 15 feet of blackboard—she endeavored to explain why they were being added. Unfortunately it was hard to see the terms from halfway back in the room, and almost impossible to hear what she was saying.*

"Finally she turned triumphantly to the class, smiled, and said something like, 'Now there—that's the complete description of . . .' The bell rang, and she departed. I was left staring at this enormously long equation about which I understood virtually nothing, although I am sure she explained every term to the blackboard as she was adding them."

"Lee and Yang had won the Nobel Prize three years earlier, and there was some sentiment that Mme. Wu should have shared it, for doing this incredibly difficult experiment at absolute vacuum near absolute zero."

At the time when Wu was a tenured full professor, other research universities, such as at Columbia, featured professors who are predominantly responsible for maintaining a research program, which occupies most of their time. Nevertheless, they often teach one course in a semester. Some professors feel it is necessary to do so in order to ensure that their graduate students know enough about the subject of their research. From the quote above, it is evident that although Wu was known for her extraordinary skills as an experimental physicist, she also had a mastery of the theoretical side as well.

During this period, Wu developed an ambitious program in experimental nuclear physics. For example, it had been learned that nuclei behave in some ways like entire atoms, but this discovery led only to more questions about the nucleus. Like atoms, nuclei can absorb energy, often reemitting the energy in a short period of time. The amount of time the nucleus existed in this excited state depends on many factors, and different theories usually predicted different results. It was becoming increasingly important to measure the lifetimes of these excited states, which were much less than a millionth of a second. Wu helped develop techniques that were able to measure nuclear lifetimes shorter than ever before—to nearly one-millionth of a millionth of a second.

Of course, there were still a lot of unknowns about nuclear forces, and shortly after her work in nuclear lifetimes, Wu helped devise a way to measure different nuclear forces by studying interactions between neutrons and the nuclei of helium. In the next year, she also helped clear up problems about X-ray emissions when the nucleus captures one of the inner electrons of an atom.

During this period in her life, Wu also became interested in muons. A muon seems to be an extra particle nature allows: It does not make up the atoms, and it is not found in any molecules. At first glance, it seems our universe would do very well without such a particle. When it is formed, as in some nuclear reaction, it does not live long, decaying into an electron and neutrinos in about two microseconds (two-millionths of a second). However, as short as a microsecond may sound, to physicists this can be a very long time. In fact, muons live millions of times longer than some other particles.

As far as nuclear interactions are concerned, muons are much like electrons; they feel the same forces the electrons do. Besides the fact that they decay, the only differences between muons and electrons are their mass—the muon is about 200 times heavier—and their magnetic moment. In the previous chapters, it was discussed how particles have magnetic dipole moments and can act as tiny magnets. The magnetic moment of the muon is about 200 times smaller than that of the electron, and Wu realized that this difference could be useful to measure different kinds of nuclear properties, properties that could not be unearthed using neutrons or electrons. In 1965, Wu published a paper with nine other authors from Columbia on the effects of muons and X-rays that further advanced the knowledge about nuclear energy levels and the physics of the nucleus.

Chinese scientists initiated the establishment of the Wu Chien-Shiung Scholarship Foundation in Taiwan. Wu is pictured at the inauguration of the foundation, on September 8, 1995. (Wu Chien Shiung Education Foundation)

This was an interesting stage in Wu's career. She had pioneered one of the most important experiments in physics. Of course, she could not have done it without her coworkers at the NBS, but it was her idea and she pushed it through. Her acclaim was spreading, and her results were quickly reaffirmed in labs across the globe. Each new substantiation of parity violation was another reminder of Wu's achievement. No one would expect a hard worker like Wu to sit back and relax, and she did not. She continued to look for new kinds of experiments and new questions in physics that might need her expert

Forces and Particles

During Wu's career, a profound change occurred regarding how physicists view interactions between particles. Mathematical equations are not enough, as physicists like to be able to visualize fundamental processes. In the 19th century, the prevailing view was that an object creates fields, and these fields exist throughout all of space. For example, the Earth has a gravitational field. This is represented, or conceptualized, by imagining straight lines emanating outward, in a radial direction (since the force is toward the Earth, these lines point inward, toward the Earth). The imaginary field lines fill all of space. When another object, say an apple in midair, resides in the field of the Earth, it reacts to the field lines by trying to follow them. An apple released from rest will follow the field lines until it hits the ground. If it already had a velocity, as if someone threw it, then it would take time before it aligns with the field lines. Electric charge also creates a field, the electromagnetic field, and other charged particles react as if they "feel" the presence of the field lines.

This is called the "classical description of forces." In the 1920s, quantum mechanics was developed, but it was not until about 1950 that the theory was fully developed. Richard Feynman, described in chapter 6, was helpful in the culmination of this theory, what is now called "quantum field theory." This view disposes of the concept of field lines. In its place, the interaction between two particles is visualized as being due to the exchange of other particles, called "virtual particles."

Imagine two ice skaters gliding along straight parallel lines on a frozen lake. If one of them throws a basketball to the other, the act hand. The physics involving muons intrigued her, and Wu continued to look for experiments that involved this singular particle.

At the time, muons were considered an exotic particle, and it was not understood just how they fit into the overall picture of elementary particles. It seemed that the muon was almost superfluous. It interacted much like the electron and did nothing other than disappear as soon as it was created. The situation was summed up by Isidor Rabi (1898–1988), chair of the physics department at Columbia from 1945 to 1949 and recipient of the Nobel Prize in

of tossing the ball forces the skater away, recoiling, as a cannon is thrown backward after firing a shell. In addition, the skater who catches the ball is also forced a little away, as he or she absorbs the momentum of the ball. In fact, the skaters could continue to toss the ball back and forth, creating essentially a "force" between them, forcing them farther and farther apart. This "exchange of particles" is how all of the fundamental forces are viewed, both repulsive and attractive. The exchange of virtual particles is said to mediate the force between particles.

The exchange particles come in two varieties, massive and massless. Massive particles are electrons, protons, and quarks. They can exist at rest, and their mass can be measured, but they can never reach the speed of light, which is 3×10^8 meters/second (186,000 miles per second). So-called massless particles also carry energy and momentum, but they travel at precisely the speed of light and can never come to rest. The kind of particles that mediate the electromagnetic force are called photons and are massless. In this model, when an electron flies past a proton, for example, the proton emits photons that are absorbed by the electron, and vice versa.

As this new model of interactions was taking hold, Feynman and other physicists realized that the weak interaction should also be described by the exchange of particles. Feynman proposed a theory that was called the "conserved vector current theory" to account for beta decay, and it did not take long for Wu to demonstrate that it was correct.

physics in 1944. His famous remark about the muon was, "Who ordered that?"

This sentiment was widespread. In her 1977 book, *Muon Physics,* Wu describes both the observational and emotional sense of this strange particle. A section named "Nature's Perversity" reads as follows:

> *According to the general laws of reactions, the positive or negative pions were expected to decay, respectively, to positrons or electrons and neutrinos. As it turns out, the above reaction is rare. Instead, the pion decays into a neutrino and a totally new particle: the muon. The existence of muons had no theoretical justification and was originally thought to be of no use. The frustration and bewilderment felt among the elementary particle physicists can best be reflected in a pungent comment by Gell-Mann and Rosenbaum (1957) in their article on "Elementary Particles": "The muon was the unwelcome baby on the doorstep, signifying the end of days of innocence. . . ."*

Wu had a more pragmatic view about the muon. Since it was in certain ways different from the electron, she reasoned, it would introduce new kinds of interactions. Instead of trying to figure out where the particle came from and how it fit into the grand scheme of things, Wu wanted to know how the muon could be used to understand nature better. Instead of dwelling on the mystery of the muon, she was looking for new areas of physics for which the muon could solve the mystery.

One such realm of physics was the growing field of muonic atoms. This strange atom is one in which an electron is replaced by a muon. The muon has the same charge of the electron and is subject to the same kinds of nuclear forces—the weak nuclear force—but since its mass and magnetic moment are different, the atom hosting a muon will behave differently from normal atoms. Wu was interested in this exotic form of matter; she wanted to know how it behaved and what could be learned from such a novel form of matter.

In 1968, it was known that muonic atoms could emit X-rays. Wu saw this as an opportunity to learn more about the structure of the nucleus, but none of the equipment at the time was sensitive enough to give the measurements that were essential to such a project. In response, Wu designed an experiment with a series of state-of-the-art detectors to measure the precise energy and angle of the X-rays that were emitted as the muon smashed into the nucleus. As a result of these experiments, the shape and distribution of the charge within the nucleus was better understood. In essence, the nucleus was better understood.

In a series of such measurements, Wu was able to describe the electric and magnetic properties of many nuclei that until now had kept their secrets buried deep. She unearthed energy levels of nuclei and was able to shed light on how the nucleus interacted with the innermost electrons of the atom. She went beyond her earlier work, which was predominately nuclear physics, to the physics describing the interactions of the nucleus with the electrons of an atom. Wu's study of the subject of muonic atoms and her long series of experiments had made her an expert in the field, and she wrote, with Vernon W. Hughes, the book *Muon Physics* in 1977.

Another Great Success

One of the most successful theories in physics is quantum electrodynamics, or QED. It envisions the force between charged particles in terms of the exchange of photons. It is successful because it accurately describes all of the experiments ever done in which electromagnetism is the force involved in the interaction. QED was so successful, in fact, that physicists began to try to mimic its theoretical underpinnings to explain other forces in nature. For example, since the electromagnetic force interchanges photons, it was surmised that the weak nuclear force could also be accounted for by an exchange of particles. The exchange particles would not be photons, but they could be viewed as creating a current between the nuclear particles.

This is the essence of the conserved vector current theory that Feynman had formulated (see sidebar). There was worldwide interest in such a theory, but no one knew if it was correct. The weak nuclear force is responsible for beta decay, and for this reason, Wu was especially interested. According to this theory, the beta rays emitted from ^{12}C and ^{12}N, radioactive forms of carbon and nitrogen, would have the same shape. This means that each substance would emit the same number of beta particles (positrons or electrons) with a given energy.

Wu realized that she could measure the beta particles coming from these nuclei, although the work would be different from anything she had done in the past. The first thing Wu had to do was redesign, once again, her spectrometer. She had to figure out the best place to put the sources and the detectors. Wu also had to be certain that stray particles did not bounce off the walls of the spectrometer, so she used other known sources of beta rays to make sure this was not an issue. She spent many weeks in her lab, preparing her equipment and testing everything she could think of. Others had already attempted this experiment, but their results were not conclusive. Wu had to be definitive. She wanted to be able to prove, or disprove, the conserved vector current.

Once the experiment was up and running, it did not take Wu long to collect the data she needed. The next step was to analyze it

Named in her honor, the Chien-Shiung Wu Memorial Hall at Southeast University
(Archives of Southeast University)

Wu at the computer-control console used in the "exotic atoms" experiment (AIP Emilio Segrè Visual Archives)

and then see if it was in accord with the theory. It was. She published a paper entitled "Experimental Test of the Conserved Vector Current Theory on the Beta Spectrum of B^{12} and N^{12}" in *Physical Review Letters* in 1963. In it, she stated: "This unique relation between the beta interaction and electrodynamics supports the conserved vector current theory."

This result was more important than simply confirming a particular theory. It confirmed that there was a new way to look at nature, a new way to understand the fundamental forces at work at the smallest levels. These forces are no longer to be viewed as having fields and incorporeal field lines emanating from the particle; instead, forces are to be understood as arising from the exchange of other particles.

Medical Science

Although Wu did not receive the Nobel Prize, she began winning most of the other important awards through the 1960s and 1970s. These are listed later in the chapter, along with a brief description of what the award is about. At this time Wu, still not content to rest upon her laurels, turned to biophysics. She began the ambitious program of investigating the essential protein in red blood cells, hemoglobin. Her experimental work detailed the structure of hemoglobin and, in particular, the electronic structure of the iron that is carried by the hemoglobin. These represent the first experiments of their kind and showed that the iron atoms are the same in both the healthy and unhealthy cells.

Wu gave many talks in the latter part of her career. (AIP Emilio Segrè Visual Archives)

Hemoglobin Studies

One of the most important functions of the human anatomy is to distribute oxygen throughout the body. This is accomplished by the red blood cells, which have a protein called "hemoglobin." Hemoglobin in humans contains four hemes, which are large molecules that each contain one iron atom. In the lungs, an oxygen atom binds with the iron. This is carried to other parts of the body where the oxygen is released.

Wu saw this process as the most fundamentally important process in the human body. She also saw an opportunity to help understand in detail how the oxygen binds to and is released from the iron. Anemia is a common disorder, one form of which is the inability of red blood cells to carry oxygen. Wu's research in this area represented a new direction, an area of research that could have direct benefits on the welfare of society. Wu appreciated this fact and took great pride in her new line of research.

It is not easy to change one's field. Wu's biophysics research, which she undertook with other researchers at Columbia, was new

Wu in her retirement (University Archives, Columbia University)

Wu receives an honorary degree from Harvard University. (AP Images)

to her, but it did not take long before she was making contributions. As she learned the new field, she began to think about the oxygen affinity of hemoglobin, that is, the power that hemoglobin has to attract oxygen. Hemoglobin with low oxygen affinity could not attract enough oxygen for the body, but it was not understood why some hemoglobin enjoyed a high oxygen affinity, while other hemoglobin suffered a low affinity.

One possibility was that the electronic structure of the iron atoms in the low affinity hemoglobin proteins differed from the high affinity proteins. But, one of her earlier publications in this field—"Electronic Structure of Fe^{2+} in Normal Hemoglobin and Its Isolated Subunits," which appeared in 1974 in the *Journal of Chemical Physics*—showed that this was not the case. An experiment by Wu demonstrated that the electronic configuration was the same for all of the iron-containing molecules. Although it was a negative result it was an important one. It ruled out a possibility that had been suspected to be the cause of the failure of hemoglobin to carry oxygen. This result prompted scientists to go on to investigate other areas.

Wu conducted a series of experiments in 1974–75 investigating hemoglobin, hoping to shed light on the dreadful disease sickle-cell anemia, a disease in which the iron-carrying red blood cells are deformed. Although she did not find a cure for this disease, Wu made significant progress in the field. By bringing her considerable expertise to bear on such an important problem and by developing new kinds of experiments to test the hemoglobin, she helped advance the field of biophysics and spurred further research of sickle-cell anemia.

Sickle-Cell Disease

The single most important ingredient to sustain life in humans is oxygen. Taking nearly 20,000 breaths each day, humans continually extract this element from the atmosphere and, through an ingenious transport system, deliver it to the cells where it is used in muscles and tissues that maintain many bodily functions.

The oxygen is introduced into the body through the lungs, where it attaches to special large molecules called "hemoglobin." The hemoglobin are like seats in a taxi, the taxis being the red blood cells. They navigate through the blood vessels until they find their destination, any of the myriad cells that need oxygen to function. The taxis do not go back to the lungs empty; they carry the waste product carbon dioxide and exchange it for oxygen in the lungs.

Healthy red blood cells are shaped like doughnuts, except that instead of having a hole in the center, there is a thin connecting region. This shape allows them to travel easily throughout the bloodstream, even through the constricted regions where the blood vessels become narrow. In the sickle-cell disease, or sickle-cell anemia, the red blood cells are misshapen. They are in the shape of a C, or a sickle. This shape prevents their free movement through the blood vessels. They often get blocked and cannot make it through to all of the cells and muscles. The result is that a person with sickle-cell disease is often tired from lack of oxygen or in pain from blockage of a blood vessel due to the poorly shaped red blood cells.

Sickle-cell disease is inherited, resulting from the genetic alteration of the amino acids that are contained in hemoglobin. Wu

During this period, as Wu's retirement in 1980 neared, she accelerated her travel schedule. She went around the world, sometimes talking about her work but also promoting women in science. She visited her homeland, where she was dubbed the "Madame Curie of China," as well as many universities across the United States. By letting young people, and especially young women, see that she could succeed in her competitive profession, she hoped to inspire them to succeed. To this day, physics is a science dominated by men, but Wu did indeed inspire more women to join the field.

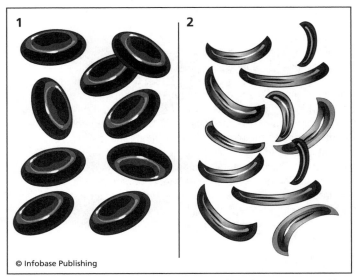

© Infobase Publishing

Normal red blood cells are shown on the left. Cells from a person with sickle-cell disease are shown on the right.

turned her attention to the study of hemoglobin in order to help understand the causes and perhaps find a cure, or prevention, of this disease.

Honors

The following is a chronological list of honors bestowed upon Wu for her outstanding successes in research and her exemplary career as a nuclear physicist.

1958: Elected member of the National Academy of Sciences
For scientists, this is the most prestigious organization in the United States. As stated on the academy's Web site (http://www.nasonline. org/site/PageServer), "Members and foreign associates are elected annually in recognition of their distinguished achievements in original research; election is considered one of the highest honors that can be accorded a scientist or engineer."

1958: Research Corporation Award
The Research Corporation for Science Advancement is a private foundation that provides funding for research, usually at a university. The funding is extremely competitive. According to the mission statement, "Research Corporation . . . provides catalytic and opportunistic funding for innovative scientific research and development of academic scientists, which will have a lasting impact on science and society." On January 22, 1958, the Research Corporation held a dinner in Wu's honor and presented her with the award. The citation for the award read: "The Research Corporation Award for 1958 is presented to Chien-shiung Wu in recognition of her crucial contributions to the major advances during the last ten years in understanding beta-decay and the weak interactions. Especially for the first clear experimental demonstration, through beta-decay of oriented nuclei, of the violation of parity conservation, long considered a fundamental law of nature. This demonstration has stimulated new and perceptive inquiries into the properties of the mesons and has given hope of a more basic understanding of the elementary particles."

1959: Achievement Award, American Association of University Women
This award recognizes the greatest achievements of university women. According to the association's Web site (http://www.aauw. org/), "One of the world's largest sources of funding exclusively for graduate women, the AAUW Educational Foundation supports aspiring scholars around the globe, teachers and activists in local communities, women at critical stages of their careers, and those pursuing professions where women are underrepresented."

1964: Comstock Award
This extremely competitive award, presented only once every five years by the National Academy of Sciences, is bestowed to a resident of North America for recent innovative discovery or investigation in electricity, magnetism, or radiant energy. Ernest Lawrence also won this award in 1938 for his development of the cyclotron.

1965: Chi-Tsin Achievement Award
The Chi-Tsin Culture Foundation of Taiwan presented this award to Wu for her work in beta decay and parity.

1968: Honorary Fellow Royal Society of Edinburgh

1973: Appointment as the first Michael I. Pupin Professor of Physics, Columbia University

1973: Head of the American Physical Society
Wu was the first woman to hold this esteemed position.

1974: Scientist of the Year Award
This is bestowed by *Industrial Research* magazine.

1975: Tom Bonner Prize
It is awarded by the American Physical Society, according to its Web site (http://www.aps.org/programs/honors/prizes/index.cfm), "To recognize and encourage outstanding experimental research in nuclear physics, including the development of a method, technique, or device that significantly contributes in a general way to nuclear physics research."

1975: (U.S.) National Medal of Science
According to the National Science Foundation's Web site (http://www.nsf.gov/od/nms/medal.jsp), "The National Medal of Science was established by the 86th Congress in 1959 as a Presidential Award to be given to individuals deserving of special recognition by reason of their outstanding contributions to knowledge in the physical, biological, mathematical, or engineering sciences."

1978: Wolf Prize in Physics
The first-ever Wolf Foundation award went to Wu in 1978. Physicists around the world regard this as the most prestigious award in physics, excepting the Nobel Prize in physics. According to the foundation's charter (http://www.wolffund.org.il/main.asp), its purpose is "To award prizes to outstanding scientists and artists—irrespective

(continues on next page)

(continued from previous page)

of nationality, race, color, religion, sex or political views—for achievements in the interest of mankind and friendly relations among peoples."

1990: Asteroid 2752 Wu Chien-shiung
The Chinese Academy of Science named asteroid 2752 after Wu, the first living scientist to hold such honor.

1991: Pupin Medal
This is the most prestigious award from Columbia University's School of Engineering. According to the university Web site (http://www.columbia.edu/cu/news/05/11/elgeston_medal.html), "It was created by the Columbia Engineering School Alumni Association in 1958 to commemorate the centenary of the birth of Michael I. Pupin (1858–1935), physicist, inventor and professor of electro-mechanics at Columbia from 1901 to 1931." The award is presented periodically.

   *: **Fellow American Academy of Arts and Sciences**

   *: **Fellow American Association for the Advancement of Science**

   *: **Fellow American Physical Society**
To become a Fellow in the above groups, one must be nominated by persons in that group and then approved. Fellows are recognized for outstanding contributions in the field of physics.

Honorary Degrees:

- Doctor of Science (D.Sc.) degrees awarded by Princeton University (1958), Smith College (1959), Goucher College (1960), Rutgers University (1961), Yale University (1967), Russell Sage College (1971), Harvard University (1974), Bard College (1974), Adelphi University (1974), and Dickinson College (1975)

- Doctor of Laws (LL.D.) degree awarded by Chinese University, Hong Kong (1969)

Wu never forgot her roots and at this time, became more interested in helping develop science in China. Noemie Koller, her student from the 1960s, gave a talk at the 1997 meeting of the American

Wu (center) and her husband, Luke Yuan (far left), with colleagues (AIP Emilio Segrè Visual Archives)

Physical Society, at which she noted some of Wu's many important roles and achievements:

> *Professor Wu has led in many of the discoveries in nuclear physics in the second half of the 20th century. She has been a teacher to many a generation of nuclear and particle physicists. In her role as President of the American Physical Society, she supported the improvement of teaching physics, mathematics and science. She supported efforts to uphold the freedom of scientists elsewhere in the world. In later years, she devoted much of her time to develop the scientific infrastructure in both China and Taiwan.*

Wu had changed or altered her field of research several times throughout her career, but her foray into biophysics would be her last. In 1997, at the age of 84, Wu died in New York after suffering a stroke.

Conclusion

Change came quick to Chien-shiung Wu. She left her hometown of Liu Ho after the fifth grade, traveling to the larger city of Suchou for further education. After she finished college in China, she sailed halfway around the world to Berkeley and moved on again soon after she received her Ph.D. This time, she went across the country, to New England and New Jersey, finally settling at Columbia University in New York City.

The geographical changes were necessary for Wu. They enabled her to pursue her dream of learning physics, the subject she loved since her childhood days in China. And, the dream came true. As she learned the field she loved dearly, Wu began making contributions to that field. She was invited to work on the secret Manhattan Project, where she made significant contributions to the war effort and began making improvements in the equipment used to measure radioactive materials. That was only the beginning, and, as this volume explained, Wu went on to make many important contributions in physics.

Following her calling was not easy. Besides leaving her homeland and family, Wu had to stand up against discrimination against women and Asians. As she worked in her lab and as she taught classes, her remarkable abilities allowed her to overcome these impediments. Her talent and work ethic also allowed her to examine some of the most important problems of the time. Nuclear physics was still in its adolescence, and Wu's contributions helped shape the world in which we live today.

In her most famous experiment, explained in chapter 6, Wu showed that parity is not conserved, bringing about a revolution in physics. After nearly four decades of holding a firm belief that parity is conserved, Wu burst a dam of ignorance, allowing a flood of new physics to flow. This enabled physicists to understand the true nature of nuclear forces. Her work in nuclear physics paved the way for the current understanding of how elementary particles behave.

As soon as Wu arrived in the United States, she was struck with the inequality between men and woman. She did not let this deter her, but later in her career, Wu took up the fight against these injustices. In China, as a young student, she had lived up to her name, Courageous Hero, when she led a student protest against General Chiang Kai-shek. As her successful career in physics was coming to an end, Wu participated in another struggle, the fight to get more women involved in science. She was elected as president of American Physical Society and used that position to promote physics to women. She traveled to different countries and lectured across the United States, her very presence showing that women can succeed in science.

Although she died of a stroke on February 18, 1997, in Manhattan, Wu lives on through her students and her work. Beyond the actual results she obtained, Wu set the standard for carrying out excellent experimental physics research and experimentation. Her methods were the best of the time, and she carefully considered every possible effect that could alter the outcome of an experiment. From the very blueprint of the experiments to the way she collected the data, she showed how to design experiments. Her extremely high standards are still with us, a legacy that will never die.

CHRONOLOGY

....

1911   Ernest Rutherford discovers the true structure of the atom, which contains a tiny nucleus, giving birth to nuclear physics. In China, the Revolution of 1911 occurs, ending the dynasties.

1912   Wu Chien-shiung (Wu Jianxong, or Chien-shiung Wu in English) is born, May 13, in China.

1914   James Chadwick discovers beta decay—electrons emitted from the nucleus.

1927   Eugene Wigner proves parity is conserved in electromagnetic interactions.

1928   Chien-shiung Wu graduates from high school in Suchou (Suzhou) and is accepted at the National Central University.

1931   Ernest Lawrence, at Berkeley, invents and builds the cyclotron, an instrument used to accelerate particles to very high speeds.

1933   Enrico Fermi develops the theory of beta decay.

1934   Chien-shiung Wu graduates from National Central University and works in crystallography.

1936   Chien-shiung Wu sails to California and becomes a graduate student at Berkeley.

1939   Japan invades China, cutting off Chien-shiung Wu from her family.

1940   Chien-shiung Wu earns her Ph.D. in physics from Berkeley.

The Manhattan Project begins.

1941–45 The United States fights in World War II.

1942 Chien-shiung Wu marries Luke Chia-liu Yuan, moves east, and takes a position at Smith College.

1943 Chien-shiung Wu moves to Princeton and becomes the university's first female instructor.

1944 Chien-shiung Wu begins work for the Manhattan Project and joins Columbia University as a research scientist.

1947 Chien-shiung Wu's son, Vincent Yuan, is born.

1948 Chien-shiung Wu solves a major problem in beta decay and proves Enrico Fermi's theory.

1950 Chien-shiung Wu's experiment shows two kinds of beta decay.

1952 Chien-shiung Wu becomes associate professor at Columbia University.

1953 Controversy around decay of radium is settled by Chien-shiung Wu's experiment.

1956 In her most famous experiment, Chien-shiung Wu proves that parity is not conserved.

1957 *New York Times* headline announces parity is not conserved. Chien-shiung Wu and coworkers publish their result.

Tsung-Dao Lee and Chen Ning Yang receive Nobel Prize for suggesting parity is not conserved. Wu is left out of recognition.

1958 Chien-shiung Wu becomes full professor at Columbia University, is elected to the National Academy of Sciences, and wins the Research Corporation Award.

1959 Chien-shiung Wu wins the Achievement Award from the American Association of University Women.

1960s   Chien-shiung Wu begins research on exotic matter, atoms containing muons.

1963   Chien-shiung Wu proves the conserved vector current theory is the correct description of beta decay.

1964   National Academy of Sciences awards Chien-shiung Wu the Comstock Award.

1965   Chien-shiung Wu wins the Chi-Tsin Achievement Award.

1970s   Changing fields, Chien-shiung Wu begins to work in biophysics.

1973   Chien-shiung Wu is appointed the first Michael I. Pupin Professor of Physics at Columbia University and is elected to head the American Physical Society.

1974   Chien-shiung Wu receives Scientist of the Year Award and publishes her work on sickle-cell disease.

1975   Chien-shiung Wu is awarded the Tom Bonner Prize in nuclear physics and receives the National Medal of Science

1978   Chien-shiung Wu wins the Wolf Prize in physics.

1980   Chien-shiung Wu retires.

1990   The Chinese Academy of Science names asteroid 2752 after Chien-shiung Wu.

1991   Chien-shiung Wu wins the Pupin Medal.

1997   Chien-shiung Wu dies of a stroke in New York.

GLOSSARY

absolute zero   the coldest temperature; it can be approached but never reached.

adiabatic demagnetization   a method to reach temperatures as low as one-thousandth of a degree kelvin

alpha ray or **particle**   a ray that consists of the nucleus of the helium atom, two protons and two neutrons

amino acid   a molecule that joins with other amino acids to form proteins, which build muscle tissue

amorphous   not in any order, random

anemia   a condition in which the red blood cells cannot carry oxygen

angstrom   one ten-billionth of a meter

antiparticle   a particle with the opposite charge and spin but same mass as a given particle

atom   the smallest unit of any element, consisting of a much smaller nucleus (made of protons and neutrons) and electrons further away

beta decay   the emission of electrons from a nucleus

beta ray   an electron

cobalt   a metal that has radioactive isotopes

conserved current theory   a theoretical description of beta decay

continuous spectrum   a continuous band of light with all colors present, such as a rainbow

crystal   the uniform, ordered array of atoms in a lattice

cyclotron   a machine used to accelerate subatomic particles to high speeds

diffraction pattern   the bright and dark areas observed when X-rays are sent through a crystal

discrete spectrum   radiated light that contains certain, distinct colors

evaporative cooling   a method to reduce temperature below one degree kelvin

excited state   the condition when an atom or nucleus has extra energy that it soon emits

fermi   a unit of distance, 10^{-15} meters

Feynman diagrams   pictorial sketches that indicate particular kinds of interaction between particles

fission   the breaking up of nuclei, a process that gives off vast energy

fissionable   capable of undergoing fission; uranium is fissionable.

fusion   the process whereby small nuclei come together, making a larger nucleus

gamma ray   particle of light, photon

half-life   the amount of time it takes for half of the number of atoms to decay

hemoglobin   an important protein in red blood cells, which carry oxygen from the lungs to other parts of the body

inner electron   an electron closest to the nucleus in an atom

ionize   to add or remove electrons from an atom

isotope   a different form of the same nucleus, varying by the number of neutrons it contains

linear accelerator   straight, tunnel-shaped apparatus used to accelerate charged particles to very high speeds

magnetic moment   the inherent property of subatomic particles to give rise to magnetic fields

meson   a short-lived particle made from a quark and antiquark

modern physics   physics after 1900, which includes quantum mechanics

muon   a particle similar to an electron but more massive; it decays.

muonic atom   an atom that contains a muon

neutrino   a subatomic particle emitted during beta decay

nucleus   the center of an atom, containing neutrons and protons and much smaller than the atom itself

parity   a property of elementary particles that makes their mirror image identical to the particles themselves

pion   a pi meson, a quark-antiquark pair

polarization   the direction of the electric field of light

positron   an antielectron

quantum electrodynamics   a theory describing the interaction of light with matter in which light consists of discrete particles called photons

quantum mechanics   the physics of atoms and nuclei, where energy is not continuous but comes in discrete units

quark   the building block of protons and neutrons

radioactivity   the process whereby nuclei emit particles or energy

sickle-cell disease or **sickle-cell anemia**   a disease characterized by misshapen red blood cells, whose C shape inhibits their flow through the blood vessels

spectrometer   a device used to measure the speed or energy of particles

spin   property of elementary particles that makes them appear to spin like a top

theta meson and **tau meson**   once thought to be different particles, they are really the same, now called the **K-meson.**

uranium   heavy element, used in the atomic bomb

virtual particle   a particle that exists for a brief period to account for the force between other particles

X-ray   a form of electromagnetic radiation, with a shorter wavelength than visible light

Periodic Table of the Elements

1 IA																		18 VIIIA
1 H 1.00794	2 IIA											13 IIIA	14 IVA	15 VA	16 VIA	17 VIIA		2 He 4.0026
3 Li 6.941	4 Be 9.0122											5 B 10.81	6 C 12.011	7 N 14.0067	8 O 15.9994	9 F 18.9984		10 Ne 20.1798
11 Na 22.9898	12 Mg 24.3051	3 IIIB	4 IVB	5 VB	6 VIB	7 VIIB	8 VIIIB	9 VIIIB	10 VIIIB	11 IB	12 IIB	13 Al 26.9815	14 Si 28.0855	15 P 30.9738	16 S 32.067	17 Cl 35.4528		18 Ar 39.948
19 K 39.0938	20 Ca 40.078	21 Sc 44.9559	22 Ti 47.867	23 V 50.9415	24 Cr 51.9962	25 Mn 54.938	26 Fe 55.845	27 Co 58.9332	28 Ni 58.6934	29 Cu 63.546	30 Zn 65.409	31 Ga 69.723	32 Ge 72.61	33 As 74.9216	34 Se 78.96	35 Br 79.904		36 Kr 83.798
37 Rb 85.4678	38 Sr 87.62	39 Y 88.906	40 Zr 91.224	41 Nb 92.9064	42 Mo 95.94	43 Tc (98)	44 Ru 101.07	45 Rh 102.9055	46 Pd 106.42	47 Ag 107.8682	48 Cd 112.412	49 In 114.818	50 Sn 118.711	51 Sb 121.760	52 Te 127.60	53 I 126.9045		54 Xe 131.29
55 Cs 132.9054	56 Ba 137.328	57-70 ☆	72 Hf 178.49	73 Ta 180.948	74 W 183.84	75 Re 186.207	76 Os 190.23	77 Ir 192.217	78 Pt 195.08	79 Au 196.9655	80 Hg 200.59	81 Tl 204.3833	82 Pb 207.2	83 Bi 208.9804	84 Po (209)	85 At (210)		86 Rn (222)
87 Fr (223)	88 Ra (226)	89-102 ★	104 Rf (261)	105 Db (262)	106 Sg (266)	107 Bh (262)	108 Hs (263)	109 Mt (268)	110 Ds (271)	111 Rg (272)	112 Uub (285)	113 Uut (284)	114 Uuq (285)	115 Uup (288)	116 Uuh (292)	117 Uus (?)		118 Uuo (?)

☆ Lanthanoids

57 La 138.9055	58 Ce 140.115	59 Pr 140.908	60 Nd 144.24	61 Pm (145)	62 Sm 150.36	63 Eu 151.966	64 Gd 157.25	65 Tb 158.9253	66 Dy 162.500	67 Ho 164.9303	68 Er 167.26	69 Tm 168.9342	70 Yb 173.04	71 Lu 174.967

★ Actinoids

89 Ac (227)	90 Th 232.0381	91 Pa 231.036	92 U 238.0289	93 Np (237)	94 Pu (244)	95 Am 243	96 Cm (247)	97 Bk (247)	98 Cf (251)	99 Es (252)	100 Fm (257)	101 Md (258)	102 No (259)	103 Lr (260)

Atomic number — Symbol — Atomic weight

3 Li 6.941

Metals
Non-metals
Metalloids
Unknown

Numbers in parentheses are atomic mass numbers of most stable isotopes.

The Chemical Elements

(g) none / (c) nonmetallics

element	symbol	a.n.
carbon	C	6
hydrogen	H	1

(g) chalcogen / (c) nonmetallics

element	symbol	a.n.
oxygen	O	8
polonium	Po	84
selenium	Se	34
sulfur	S	16
tellurium	Te	52
ununhexium	Uuh	116

(g) alkali metal / (c) metallics

element	symbol	a.n.
cesium	Cs	55
francium	Fr	87
lithium	Li	3
potassium	K	19
rubidium	Rb	37
sodium	Na	11

(g) alkaline earth metal / (c) metallics

element	symbol	a.n.
barium	Ba	56
beryllium	Be	4
calcium	Ca	20
magnesium	Mg	12
radium	Ra	88
strontium	Sr	38

(g) none / (c) metallics

element	symbol	a.n.
aluminum	Al	13
bohrium	Bh	107
cadmium	Cd	48
chromium	Cr	24
cobalt	Co	27
copper	Cu***	29
darmstadtium	Ds	110
dubnium	Db	105
gallium	Ga	31
gold	Au***	79
hafnium	Hf	72
hassium	Hs	108
indium	In	49
iridium	Ir****	77
iron	Fe	26
lawrencium	Lr	103
lead	Pb	82
lutetium	Lu	71
manganese	Mn	25
meitnerium	Mt	109
mercury	Hg	80
molybdenum	Mo	42
nickel	Ni	28
niobium	Nb	41
osmium	Os****	76
palladium	Pd****	46
platinum	Pt****	78
rhenium	Re	75
rhodium	Rh****	45
roentgenium	Rg	111
ruthenium	Ru****	44
rutherfordium	Rf	104
scandium	Sc	21
seaborgium	Sg	106
silver	Ag***	47
tantalum	Ta	73
technetium	Tc	43
thallium	Tl	81
titanium	Ti	22
tin	Sn	50
tungsten	W	74
ununbium	Uub	112
ununtrium	Uut	113
ununquadium	Uuq	114
vanadium	V	23
yttrium	Y	39
zinc	Zn	30
zirconium	Zr	40

(g) pnictogen / (c) metallics

element	symbol	a.n.
arsenic	As*	33
antimony	Sb*	51
bismuth	Bi	83
nitrogen	N**	7
phosophorus	P**	15
ununpentium	Uup	115

(g) none / (c) semimetallics

element	symbol	a.n.
boron	B	5
germanium	Ge	32
silicon	Si	14

(g) actinoid / (c) metallics

element	symbol	a.n.
actinium	Ac	89
americium	Am	95
berkelium	Bk	97
californium	Cf	98
curium	Cm	96
einsteinium	Es	99
fermium	Fm	100
mendelevium	Md	101
neptunium	Np	93
nobelium	No	102
plutonium	Pu	94
protactinium	Pa	91
thorium	Th	90
uranium	U	92

(g) halogens / (c) nonmetallics

element	symbol	a.n.
astatine	At*	85
bromine	Br	35
chlorine	Cl	17
fluorine	F	9
iodine	I	53
ununseptium	Uus*	117

(g) lanthanoid / (c) metallics

element	symbol	a.n.
cerium	Ce	58
dysprosium	Dy	66
erbium	Er	68
europium	Eu	63
gadolinium	Gd	64
holmium	Ho	67
lanthanum	La	57
neodymium	Nd	60
praseodymium	Pr	59
promethium	Pm	61
samarium	Sm	62
terbium	Tb	65
thulium	Tm	69
ytterbium	Yb	70

(g) noble gases / (c) nonmetallics

element	symbol	a.n.
argon	Ar	18
helium	He	2
krypton	Kr	36
neon	Ne	10
radon	Rn	86
xenon	Xe	54
unococtium	Uuo	118

a.n. = atomic number
(g) = group
(c) = classification

* = semimetallics (c)
** = nonmetallics (c)
*** = coinage metal (g)
**** = precious metal (g)

FURTHER RESOURCES

Books

Cooperman, Stephanie. *Chien-Shiung Wu: Pioneering Physicist and Atomic Researcher.* New York: Rosen, 2004.

> For young readers, this book describes problems and hardships Wu faced in the United States.

Friedman, Robert Marc. *The Politics of Excellence: Behind the Nobel Prize in Physics.* New York: W. H. Freeman, 2001.

> Although this book does not mention Wu specifically, it discusses the politics behind winning the Nobel Prize in physics.

Gamov, George. *One, Two, Three, Infinity.* New York: Dover, 1947.

> A witty and humorous book about physics.

Howes, Ruth, and Caroline L. Hersenberg. *Their Day in the Sun.* New York: Rosen, 2004.

> This gives accounts of Wu's interaction with coworkers and describes the atmosphere when Wu arrived in the United States.

Hughes, Vernon, and Chien-shiung Wu, eds. *Muon Physics.* New York: Academic Press, 1977.

> Although a technical book, Wu describes some of her feelings about the muon and its role in physics.

McGrayne, Sharon Bertsch. *Nobel Prize Women in Science: Their Lives, Struggles, and Momentous Discoveries.* 2d ed. Washington, D.C.: Joseph Henry Press & National Academy of Sciences, 2001.

> This describes personal aspects of Wu's life, including early friendships, and provides quotes from people who knew her.

Newman, Harvey B., and Thomas Ypsilantis, eds. *History of Original Ideas and Basic Discoveries in Particle Physics.* New York: Springer, 1996.

Written mostly for scientists, chapter 6 gives a personal account of Wu's most famous discovery of parity violation.

Reynolds, Moira Davidson. *American Women Scientists.* Jefferson, N.C.: MacFarland, 2004.

This describes Wu's early years in the United States.

Yost, Edna. *Women of Modern Science.* New York: Dodd, Mead, 1959.

This contains material about Wu leading up to her 1956 experiment on parity.

Internet Resources

Columbia 250. "Chien-Shiung Wu." Available online. URL: http://c250. columbia.edu/c250_celebrates/remarkable_columbians/chien-shiung_ wu.html. Accessed November 15, 2008.

Here is a brief but good review of Wu's life and accomplishments.

Dicke, William. "Chien-Shiung Wu, 84, Top Experimental Physicist." *New York Times* (February 18, 1997). Available online. URL: http://www. hep.caltech.edu/~hitlin/wuobit.html. Accessed November 1, 2008.

This obituary of Wu gives a succinct account of some of her major accomplishments.

Koller, Naomi. "Personal Memories of Chien-Shiung Wu." APS Forum on Physics and Society (July 1997). Available online. URL: http:// www.aps.org/units/fps/newsletters/1997/july/ajul97.html#a1. Accessed November 14, 2008.

Koller was one of Wu's graduate students who went on to become a dean at Rutgers University. This article gives a personal account of what is was like to work with Wu.

NIST Physics Laboratory. "The Fall of Parity." NIST Virtual Museum. Available online. URL: http://physics.nist.gov/GenInt/Parity/cover. html. Accessed November 15, 2008.

This is a nice account of Wu's famous experiment, with pictures of all major participants.

Sutton, Christine. "Rooted in Symmetry: Yang Reflects on a Life of Physics." *CERN Courier* (June 30, 2007). Available online. URL: http:// cerncourier.com/cws/article/cern/29815. Accessed November 1, 2008.

This article, about Chen Ning Yang, one of the physicists who seriously questioned the conservation of parity, contains quotes about Wu and her belief in the importance of doing her famous experiment.

TheBestLinks.com. "Chien-Shiung Wu." Available online. URL: http://www.thebestlinks.com/Chien.MM.Shiung_Wu.html. Accessed November 15, 2008.

This Web resource has goods links to interesting things pertaining to Wu's life.

Wikipedia. "Chien-Shiung Wu." Available online. URL: http://en.wikipedia. org/wiki/Chien-Shiung_Wu. Accessed November 15, 2008.

This is a very general history of Wu's life.

Periodicals

Feldman, L., and C. S. Wu. "Interpretation of Beta-Spectra from Thick Sources." *Physical Review* 76 (1949): 697–698.

Here, Wu investigates the effects of thick sources in beta decay and verifies her hypothesis that the source must be thin.

Gell-Mann, Murray, and E. P. Rosenbaum. "Elementary Particles." *Scientific American* (July 1957): 72–86.

This article about elementary particles has a quote about muons.

Huynh, B. H., et al. "Electronic Structure of Fe^{2+} in Normal Hemoglobin and Its Isolated Subunits." *Journal of Chemical Physics* 61 (1974): 3,750–3,758.

This article, cowritten by Wu and other colleagues, represents Wu's change of fields into biophysics. Here she investigates the electronic structure of iron in hemoglobin.

Lee, Y. K., L. W. Mo, and C. S. Wu. "Experimental Test of the Conserved Vector Current Theory on the Beta Spectrum of B^{12} and N^{12}." *Physical Review Letters* 10 (1963): 253–258.

This is one of Wu's most important publications in which she proves the conserved vector current theory is the correct description of beta decay.

Wróblewski, Andrzej K. "The Downfall of Parity—the Revolution That Happened Fifty Years Ago." *Acta Physica Polonica B* 39 (2008): 251–264. Available online. URL: http://th-www.if.uj.edu.pl/acta/vol39/pdf/v39p0251.pdf. Downloaded November 1, 2008.

This contains a delightful description of the Rochester meeting when parity nonconservation was discussed and details about Wu's famous experiment of 1956.

Wu, C. S. "The Continuous X-rays Excited by the Beta-Particles of $_{15}P^{32}$." *Physical Review* 59 (1941): 481–488.

Wu in this technical article settled the debate about whether internal or external X-rays are emitted in beta decay.

Wu, C. S., and R. D. Albert. "The Beta-Ray Spectrum of Cu^{64}." *Physical Review* 75 (1949): 315–316.

In this technical article, Wu describes how she made thin radioactive sources by adding detergent to the solution.

Wu, C. S., E. Ambler, et al. "Experimental Test of Parity Conservation in Beta Decay." *Physical Review* 105 (1957): 1,413–1,415.

This is Wu's most famous publication (a technical article), proving parity is not conserved.

Wu, C. S., B. M. Rustad, et al. "The Beta-Spectrum of He^6." *Physical Review* 87 (1952): 1,140–1,141.

This is one of Wu's very few technical publications that do not determine what she was after.

Wu, C. S., and I. Shaknov. "The Angular Correlation of Scattered Annihilation Radiation." *Physical Review* 77 (1950): 136.

In this technical article, Wu proves aspects of quantum electrodynamics is correct.

INDEX

and parity 63–68,
70–73, *72*, 76–82
and Sixth Annual
Rochester
Conference 66–67
and weak interactions
67–68
Wu's initial
involvement with
68, 70
Tom Bonner Prize 101

U
uncertainty 9
University of California
at Berkeley xi, 19, 22,
24
University of Michigan
19, 22
up alignment 71
up quarks 64, *65*
up spin 45
uranium
enrichment of 34–35
fission 24, *25*
half-life 10–11
Rutherford's studies
4–6
uranium-235 (^{235}U)
10–11, 35
uranium-238 (^{238}U) 35
uranium hexafluoride
(UF$_6$) 35
Urey, Harold 34

V
variable theory of beta
decay 44
vector interaction 53, 70
virtual particles 88–89

W
waves 9
weak force
and beta decay 67, 83
and conserved
vector current
theory 91

and exchange
particles 91
and muonic atoms
90
and parity 68
weak gamma radiation
31
weak interaction 68, 70
Weinrich, Marcel 82
Weisskopf, Victor 77
white light 7
Wigner, Eugene 29,
58–59, 67
Wolf Prize in Physics
101–102
women, discrimination
against xi, 28–29, 32,
34, 105
Wooster, W. A. 15
World War II 23, 29,
36
Wu, Chien-shiung *3,
14, 19, 56, 64, 84, 87,
95–97, 103*
arrival in U.S. 19–20
at Berkeley 21–23
birth and early
childhood 1–2
birth of son 54–57
in California xi,
21–23
cancellation of 20th
anniversary cruise
73, 76
on choosing field of
research 41–42
at Columbia
University 40–44,
*43, 47, 52. See
also* Columbia
University
conserved vector
current theory
research 92–93, *93*
early education in
China 2–3
at first Mössbauer
Conference *80*

Geiger counter
improvements 37
hemoglobin research
94–98
honors awarded to
100–102
and Manhattan
Project 34–36
move to Eastern U.S.
32–34
muon research
87–91
at National Academy
of Sciences,
Shanghai 18
National Central
University of
China offer
61–62
Nobel Prize denied
to 84–86
nuclear lifetimes
measured by 86
overcoming
prejudice 28–29
on parity 59
parity experiment
76–82, *78*
particle-antiparticle
annihilation study
57–60
and science in China
102–103
at Smith College
32–33, *33*
student protests 17,
105
as teacher 34, 55,
85–86
various contributions
to particle physics
83–93
work ethic of 55–57,
76
after World War II
39–40
and xenon problem
26–27